Assault on Democracy

Matthew G. Whitaker's Attack on
Gay State Senator Matt McCoy

Iowa State Senator Matt McCoy
&
Jim Ferguson, Ph.D.

Front cover image of author Matt McCoy, portraits of McCoy on
pages i and 183 by Ben Easter,
Ben Easter Photography, Des Moines, IA.
All photos, unless otherwise noted, are from authors'
collections.

Cover Design by
Michael A. Sisti, Sarasota, FL

For my parents Bill and Mary Ann McCoy
who always believed in me and taught me to stand up
for what is right.

~~~

For my incredible wife Jill Ferguson
with thanks for decades of endless love and laughter.

Authors' Notation

Matt McCoy was an Iowa State Senator at the time
the events in this book occurred
In January 2019 McCoy was sworn in as a
Polk County (Iowa) Supervisor

Also by

Matthew W. McCoy
&
James E. Ferguson, Ph.D.

McCoy, You're Going Straight to Hell
Heartfelt Letters to a Gay State Senator on Marriage Equality

Assault on Democracy
Matthew G. Whitaker's attack on Gay State Senator Matt McCoy

Table of Contents

Preface   1

Chapter 1: Who is Matthew G. Whitaker?   5

Chapter 2: Knock on My Door   25

Chapter 3:

Not What I Expected: *Bio, Politics, Addiction, Orientation*   43

Chapter 4: What Happened   61

Chapter 5: Indictment   82

Chapter 6: Trial   114

Chapter 7: Whitaker's Assault on Democracy   140

Appendices   152

Acknowledgements   182

Authors   183

Sources Cited   185

McCoy Trial Defense Attorney Jerry Crawford

Matt McCoy showed enormous courage in the face of the federal government's baseless attack on him. Imagine being a lone citizen up against the FBI, the Public Integrity Section of the Justice Department, and the United States Attorney's Office! To say nothing of these agencies' unlimited financial resources, compared with Matt's modest means. Oh yeah, and throw in a conviction rate just north of ninety percent for good measure.

The steep odds are why the vast majority of people in Matt's situation agree to a plea bargain, regardless of whether they have done anything wrong. But not Matt.

I will never forget Matt calling me on my cell phone at 6:00 a.m. MT one weekday morning (as I tend to be an early riser) and telling me, "Jerry the FBI is here wanting to question me."

"Don't say a word," I told Matt. We were off to the races. The first call I made was to F. Montgomery ("Monty") Brown to ask for him to assist us. My fulltime criminal lawyering was in my past and I needed a criminal law specialist to back me up in Matt's case. Monty was and is the best.

From that day until the jury delivered its resounding not guilty verdict (after 25 minutes of deliberation) was a long, long slog. But Matt's determination to stand up for himself and fight the charges never wavered.

We also caught a break when the case was assigned to Federal District Court Judge James Gritzner, a man of resounding integrity who brought fairness to a process that did not start out so fair. My admiration for Matt is profound. As you will learn in the pages that follow, Matt was and is a true profile in courage.

Defense Attorney Jerry Crawford

McCoy Trial Defense Attorney F. Montgomery Brown

In over 30 years of criminal defense practice I have had the occasional client whom I thought was actually innocent. I knew Matt McCoy was innocent once I listened to the tapes and reviewed Mr. McCoy's Senate disclosures revealing his outside business activity. I have no doubt that when the FBI Agent interviewed Mr. McCoy the Agent said "what disclosures" when Mr. McCoy brought them up. My office delivered them to the U.S. Attorney's Office that same day. They knew nothing about them. The prosecution train was already rolling so they had to ignore the import of the disclosures. The prosecution's late disclosure of exculpatory evidence provided us with a trial continuance. With that continuance we located two key witnesses who helped prove Mr. McCoy's innocence. When the defense team, Mr. McCoy and his family left the courthouse after I cross-examined the informant/antagonist there was a beautiful rainbow outside. I can still see it exactly as it appeared over the State Capitol building East of the federal courthouse. It was an extraordinary moment in my career.

Defense Attorney F. Montgomery Brown

McCoy Trial Defense Attorney Jim Quilty

There is a quote etched into the ceiling of the capitol building in Des Moines that reads: "Where law ends tyranny begins." That quote should have special resonance today as we live in an era where the rule of law is being eroded by an effort to politicize the judiciary and the administration of justice in our country. The seeds for that effort took root in the early to mid-2000s and, in at least one small respect, I had the privilege of helping the effort to fight back and hold the line in support of the rule of law.

The prosecution of Matt McCoy was part of a national effort to use the Department of Justice to attack progressive leaders. The government's case was flawed in many respects. Those flaws were compounded by extreme prosecutorial misconduct. While the defense succeeded in proving Matt's innocence to the jury (the jury reached a not guilty verdict after just a mere 25 minutes of deliberation) the tremendous toll the prosecution took on Matt and his family will never be fully remedied.

I was proud to be a part of Matt's trial team and am grateful to know he has continued to serve our community as a public servant.

Defense Attorney Jim Quilty

Preface

What is found between the covers of this book is a highly personal story. It is my story. A story painfully shared as I came to terms with my past, my true identity, and the challenges foisted upon me. As an elected official this was played out in full view of the public. I struggled with alcoholism, my sexual orientation, divorce, and fought trumped-up federal charges of attempted extortion. My cherished privacy seems a small price to pay when I have the opportunity–no, the obligation–to bring strength to others coming to terms with similar struggles. I hope they will gain, as I have, the fortitude to live their lives with integrity and pride.

This book is a story about a federal witch hunt led by U.S. Attorney of the Southern District of Iowa Matthew (Matt) G. Whitaker as he sought to use any means available to break my spirit, deplete my resources, and derail my political career. Des Moines is hardly the setting for such a travesty of justice. It is a progressive well-run city where people address each other on a first name basis. Possessing integrity is their lifeline for success in business as well as relationships.

As I fought a trumped-up federal indictment and trial for attempted extortion, the real story was what was happening underneath the visible tale, which was the Department of Justice's (DOJ) misuse of its immense power. It is not a *then* story, it's a *now* story. Governmental abuse of power continues against citizens because of their politics or sexual orientation. In spite of my sterling political record, I was to learn the DOJ had extended its long arm to the country's heartland to seize my rights to privacy, threaten me with a long prison term and levy a fine that would take a lifetime to pay. It was me, Iowa State Senator Matt McCoy, who was pursued. You can very well be their next target.

For 18 months of my life, the FBI under then U.S. Attorney General Alberto Gonzales and his henchman U.S. Attorney Matthew Whitaker, stopped at nothing in their attempt to rob me of my reputation, livelihood, and most concerning, my freedom. The dissonance created in knowing what legally should be happening, but experiencing the opposite was frustrating, resulting in unending anguish. So many times, I thought, "You can't do that." Apparently, the DOJ had not read the same Constitution that I, as a State Senator, had sworn to preserve.

What I thought was just my small isolated business deal gone sour, slowly unraveled into a greater understanding that it was linked to a strategy occurring across the country. I now believe I was one of the Democrats at the grassroots level that U.S. Attorney General Alberto Gonzales, with the support of Matt Whitaker, targeted in their reign of terror on elected Democrats. Karl Rove was credited with having conceived this plan. His goal was simple: create a permanent majority of Republicans in America by eroding support for Democrats.

This is not merely a self-serving rationale for what happened to me. A 2007 a study by Shields & Cragan found that U.S. attorneys investigated seven times as many Democratic elected officials as Republicans in order to disrupt the Democratic Party at the grassroots. It provided the evidence of why the DOJ was interested in me and other Democratic elected officials.

What role did my sexual orientation play in this? I'm an outspoken advocate for gay rights. I played a significant role in defeating a proposed Iowa constitutional amendment banning gay marriage. I worked for Senate confirmation of an openly gay man to the Iowa State Board of Education. And additionally, through my efforts, the State allocated $400,000 to an AIDS project that provided life-saving drugs for AIDS patients. Most recently, I successfully promoted legislation prohibiting the bullying of gays in schools and prohibiting discrimination of gays in housing and the workplace. Many people thought my being openly gay was a contributing factor in my being an easy target to be prosecuted by the feds. Nationally, I had been named a rising star in the Democratic Party.

I tried to live my life honestly while addressing highly personal challenges. In doing so, I shared my struggles with constituents. Consequently, I have the distinction, or notoriety, of being Iowa's highest ranking *openly* gay elected official. This distinction was not something I actually sought. After I came out, I went on to win re-elections to the Iowa Senate. I also won election to the Polk County Board of Supervisors by an 82% majority.

My story is important because the American people need to know about the assault on our democracy by the heavy-handed

U.S. Department of Justice. The Department of Justice, with unlimited resources, can destroy innocent individuals who often collapse under the immense weight of this persecution. I did not, and that made all the difference.

My former co-author, business associate, and trusted friend, Jim Ferguson, joins me in relating my story.

Referring to an unnamed lawyer Lincoln said,
"He can compress the most words into the smallest ideas
of any man I ever met."
Abraham Lincoln[1]

1

Who is Matthew G. Whitaker?

"Marriage should be between one man and one woman."
"Appointed judges should have a 'biblical view of justice.' If they
had a secular worldview, that would make <u>him</u> 'very concerned about
how they judge.'" [2]
Matt Whitaker

Matt Whitaker

Matthew George Whitaker was appointed June 15, 2004 by President George W. Bush as U.S. Attorney for the Southern District of Iowa. His life and mine would intersect at various points but most critically at the time of my federal indictment and trial for attempted extortion. Whitaker was the federal attorney in charge of that investigation leading to charges against me. I was his victim.

Whitaker was born October 29, 1969, and graduated from Ankeny High School (Iowa). His mother was an elementary school teacher, his father a car salesman. Whitaker graduated with a BA, MBA, and law degree from The University of Iowa where he was a starter for the Iowa Hawkeyes football team playing tight end. Whitaker is a Lutheran. His wife, Marci, is a civil engineer. They have three children.

Whitaker not an Academic All-American as claimed

"Matthew Whitaker, the acting attorney general, incorrectly claimed on his resume and on government documents that he was named an Academic All-American while he played football at The University of Iowa.

The Wall Street Journal reported: A spokeswoman for the College Sports Information Directors of America told the *Journal* that the organization doesn't have a record of Whitaker as an Academic All-American. The spokeswoman, Barb Kowal, said Whitaker appeared to have been awarded a lower honor, an All-District honor. Student athletes must have at least a 3.3 cumulative grade point average to be eligible to be nominated as an Academic All-American."[3]

Political ambitions

Driven by strong political ambitions, Whitaker ran for Iowa State Treasurer in 2002. His high aspirations ended by losing to incumbent Mike Fitzgerald. Fitzgerald happens to be the "Dean of State Treasurers," an honorary title given to the longest serving state treasurer in the nation. Fitzgerald has never lost an election. Whitaker was soundly defeated winning only 43% of the vote to Fitzgerald's 55%.

Not to be totally defeated, Whitaker was again on the ballot this time running for the U.S. Senate in 2014. He placed fourth in the primary for the seat eventually garnering only 7.54% of the votes. Joni Ernst went on to win the seat becoming Iowa's first woman U.S. senator.

"Whitaker was one of 61 candidates who applied for three spots on the Iowa Supreme Court in 2011. He arrived at his interview with his family and his minister...but he was eliminated early and was not one of the nine names advanced to Gov. Terry Branstad for consideration."[4]

Whitaker kicked off his interview by showing the Supreme Court Justices his Rose Bowl ring. He shared with them that he kept the ring in a safety deposit box, wearing it only on special occasions like his marriage. He told them that he wore the ring today to show how special he felt about the day. He went on bragging that he could have had former University of Iowa legendary Football Coach Hayden Fry there to support him but Whitaker did not want to have Fry travel all the way from Texas.

Incidentally, Whitaker wore no rings during his testifying before the House Judiciary Committee on February 8, 2019 where Senator Jerrold Nadler of New York told him that it was getting tiresome hearing him stall and waste time.

"Though Whitaker wasn't one of the nine, (candidates for the Iowa Supreme Court recommended for consideration for placement on the Court) he was willing to talk candidly about it, which isn't a popular strategy for lawyers who try cases before judges...The process, he said, is still stacked against conservatives like him...the Supreme Court's...7-0 same-sex marriage ruling shows the court lacks 'diversity of thought'...He's against same sex marriage...Some say Whitaker's problem wasn't being too conservative. It was being too political. While most candidates came with letters of support, Whitaker was one of the few who drew letters of complaint."[5]

Founder of FACT

Whitaker was the 2016 founder and executive director of the Foundation for Accountability and Civic Trust (FACT), a conservative watchdog group. FACT accused many Democrats, including Hillary Clinton, of illegal and ethical violations. It came under scrutiny when Trump named him Acting Attorney General. As its executive director, Whitaker was paid $1.5 million over a four-year period.

"During his tenure, Whitaker was one of only two people on the payroll, and he made a total of $717,000 from 2014 to 2016. Funding for that salary and all of FACT's work has come from mostly untraceable donors. Over a three-year period, FACT received $2.45 million in contributions, and all but about $450 of that came from a fund called DonorsTrust, according to IRS filings. Contributors to DonorsTrust are mostly anonymous, except for well-known conservative financier Charles Koch."[6] Ironically, the company was under an FBI investigation, during the time Whitaker served as acting Attorney General.

Other employment

Whitaker had been with the law firms of Finley Alt Smith in Des Moines and Briggs & Morgan in the Twin Cities. He was a corporate counsel for Supervalu grocery store. "He served on the advisory board of World Patent Marketing in Miami, the company that has been accused by the government of bilking millions of dollars from customers."[7] The company "was fined $26 million and shut down by the Federal Trade Commission in 2017 for deceiving consumers."[8]

Acting United States Attorney General

Whitaker served as Chief of Staff for Attorney General Jeff Sessions from September 2017 to November 2018. Following Sessions' resignation Whitaker was appointed by President Trump (November 7, 2018) as acting U.S. Attorney General. The appointment resulted in several lawsuits claiming the appointment was unconstitutional as the appointment had to be approved by the U.S. Senate.

"Matthew Whitaker is unfit to serve as acting U.S. attorney general. . .Prior to his meteoric ascent to Acting Attorney General at age 49, Mr. Whitaker owned a daycare center, a concrete supply business, and a trailer manufacturer. He spearheaded an endeavor to build affordable housing in Des Moines with government subsidies. He has ultra-thin credentials for serving as Acting Attorney General...In a question and answer interview when he sought the nomination of Senator in Iowa in 2014, Mr. Whitaker asserted: 'There are so many bad [Supreme Court] rulings. I would start with the idea of *Marbury v. Madison*. That's a good place to start...' Justice Antonin Scalia...testified at his Senate confirmation hearing: '...*Marbury* is of course one of the great pillars of American law. It is the beginning of the Supreme Court as the interpreter of the Constitution...' To the extent that you think a nominee would be so foolish, or so extreme as to kick over one of the pillars of the Constitution, I suppose you should not confirm him."[9]

A bit of a meteor

"'The guy's a bit of a meteor,' said Robert Rigg, a Drake Law School professor who got to know Whitaker in 2011 when each defended clients over a scandal involving Iowa's now-defunct film tax credit program."[10]

A prominent Des Moines lawyer opined, "Matt Whitaker is a prime example of the 'Peter Principle.'"

Satirical "thanks" for Matt Whitaker's appointment

"Mr. President, there is another reason Matthew Whitaker will make the perfect attorney general: his character. Mr. Whitaker worked for a company that is under FBI investigation and that the Federal Trade Commission said 'bilked thousands of consumers out of millions of dollars.' Now, at first blush that does not look so good. But, what Mr. Whitaker did for the company is pretty impressive. He used his position as a former U.S. attorney in Iowa to get business for the company, before it was charged with fraud by the FTC. That's pretty savvy, if you ask me. Mr. Whitaker also routinely slapped down complaints by customers who were ignored after the company took their money. In a letter to one wronged customer, Mr. Whitaker announced he was a former federal prosecutor and threatened 'serious civil and criminal consequences' if the customer went to the Better Business Bureau. I'm sure the thousands of federal prosecutors who now report to Mr. Whitaker will see this type of blatant threat not as thuggish but as an ingenious way to use public service for personal gain."[11]

Former U.S. Attorney in Iowa unimpressed

"One of his Democratic predecessors in the U.S. attorney's office in Iowa, called his career 'spectacularly unimpressive. It seems to me that it would be hard to find someone less qualified to be the attorney general, acting or not, of the United States of America,' said Roxanne Conlin, who was U.S. attorney under President Jimmy Carter and later ran unsuccessfully for governor and the U.S. Senate."[12]

Iowa Democrats furious about case against McCoy

"'He (*Whitaker*) considers law and politics full contact sports so when he quote unquote puts on the pads and goes into what he perceives as a game, 'He can be aggressive,' Rigg said." *(Robert Rigg, Drake Law School professor)*."[13]

But contact sports can leave bruises.

"Iowa Democrats are furious about an attempted extortion case Whitaker's office led against state Senator Matt McCoy over a decade ago. The jury deliberated a short time before acquitting McCoy, a Democrat and the first openly gay member of the Iowa Legislature, on all counts in 2007. McCoy said he considers it a political prosecution and recently wrote a column in *Politico* calling the case a 'witch hunt.'"[14]

McCoy: Whitaker ill-qualified to become acting A.G.

"State Sen. Matt McCoy, D-Des Moines, who was prosecuted and acquitted on a federal extortion charge in 2007 while Whitaker was U.S. attorney in Des Moines, said he can't think of a more ill-qualified person to become acting attorney general. McCoy is a Democrat and said he strongly believes the federal case brought against him was politically motivated.

McCoy said Wednesday he 'absolutely' believes Whitaker will try to subvert Mueller's investigation of Russian meddling in the 2016 presidential election. 'I think he will be very dangerous in that role,' McCoy said. 'It is beyond me how he could have risen to such a high rank. Trump needs a patsy and he will get it with Whitaker.'

McCoy was accused of trying to use his influence as a senator to force a business partner to pay him $2,000. But a federal jury deliberated less than two hours *(actually they reached their verdict in 25 minutes and then went to lunch)* before returning its verdict of not guilty.

Whitaker, now 48, had denied assertions of political motivation for pursuing the case. He issued a statement after the verdict that said he had complete confidence in the jury system and he accepted McCoy's acquittal."[15]

Role of U.S. Attorneys?

Whitaker can't be dismissed as "unintelligent." I think that would be an overreach serving no purpose. But I do think he's politically naïve. In fact, he was reported saying on the local CBS news affiliate, that prior to being appointed U.S. Attorney that he didn't even know what a U.S. Attorney did. That was coming from a law school graduate. It was an embarrassment to the United States of America, the U.S. Department of Justice, and to any intelligent, educated person in this country. As the saying goes, *"At first I couldn't even spell 'U.S. Attorney', now I is one."*

Nix on emceeing Christian sponsored dinner

Whitaker is a self-proclaimed Christian conservative. Whitaker publicly talked about being denied by his superiors his request to emcee an event for the Iowa Christian Alliance, formerly called the Iowa Christian Coalition. This was a Christian conservative, moral majority, right wing event being held in Des Moines. Whitaker wanted to headline the dinner to promote himself as a potential political candidate for public office. The Department of Justice, having received complaints about his involvement in this event and also being under scrutiny for their devious underhanded attempt to dismantle the Democratic Party at its base, forbid him from heading the event. He could however attend. He failed to see how his image as an impartial United States Attorney would be jeopardized by performing a key role at that dinner. Not only was it inappropriate, it could be risky if he was to claim impartiality in his involvement in future cases.

Judges must have biblical view of justice to be confirmed

Whitaker participated in the Christian conservative Family Leader Debate in 2014, as Whitaker was campaigning to capture the U.S. Senate nomination in Iowa.[16] Whitaker elaborated that in assisting the confirmation of judges: "'I'd like to see things like their worldview, what informs them. Are they people of faith? Do they have a [New Testament] biblical view of justice?—which I think is very important. And what I know is as long as they have that worldview, that they'll be a good judge. And if they have a secular worldview, then I'm going to be very concerned about how they judge.'

The First Amendment also protects the free exercise of religion. In *Torcasco v. Watkins* (1961), the Supreme Court declared unconstitutional a requirement that persons declare a belief in the existence of God as a condition of holding public office.

Mr. Whitaker, however, has declared that judicial nominees should be vetted based on whether they have a New Testament biblical view of justice.

In sum, he is no more fit to serve as acting attorney general as would be an atheist to serve as the Pope."[17]

DOJ fires eight attorneys

Let's look at other incidents similar to mine that were occurring at this time around the country. This will give you the political context within which I was pursued by the FBI and later wrongly indicted. This is important as it will document that what happened to me was not an isolated incident.

I did not realize for some time the full implications that what was happening to me was linked to the national scene. A national story broke that U.S. Attorney General Alberto Gonzales had fired eight U.S. prosecutors. These prosecutors were all held in good standing with the Department of Justice. The Judiciary Committees in both the House and Senate questioned what caused these firings. Did politics play a role? While these discussions were going on, some of the fired U.S. prosecutors revealed they had been approached by the Department of Justice to investigate certain individuals and to ignore others. Fired prosecutor David Iglesia, officed in Albuquerque, was articulate and outspoken as he told his story. The chair of the New Mexico Republican Party complained to Karl Rove that Iglesia failed to indict New Mexico State Senator Manny Aragon on fraud and conspiracy charges. Rove said he's fired Iglesia for performance related issues. Department of Justice's Inspector General later found that Iglesias had been wrongfully dismissed because he had refused to pursue prosecutions against the Democrat-linked community organization ACORN and a prominent New Mexico Democrat.[18] I began to see a pattern in which I too was undoubtedly a victim.

When I started looking into the DOJ and specifically the Department of Public Integrity as it related to elected officials, I learned that the Department of Public Integrity had been beefed-up under the Bush Administration as a means of trying to root out elected officials who misused their positions or political power for personal gain or privilege. This department had been in essence tripled in size and funding. It was now was under the watchful eyes of a very corrupt, biased U.S. Attorney General Alberto Gonzalez. He had been President Bush's Attorney General in Texas. Gonzalez helped Bush beat his alleged cocaine charges and his DWI in the great state of Texas. At this point we knew the kind of character with whom we were dealing. We also knew at that time Alberto Gonzales was "in bed" with Karl Rove who engineered the effort to undermine the Democratic Party at its very base. He did this by attacking Democratic elected officials throughout the country. No two "attacks" were in the same U.S. attorney's hometown. Each case was treated as an isolated instance that was only of local interest. Thus, it stayed under the national radar. That's how this mid-western boy got brought into a political scandal by a corrupt administration conducting devious and damaging campaigns against elected Democratic officials. As this effort began to unravel on a national scene it allowed us to peer into what was happening.

Politicization of the Justice Department

"Most of the eight dismissed prosecutors came from swing states, and Democrats suspect they may have been purged to make room for prosecutors who would help Republicans win close elections. If so, it might also mean that United States attorneys in all swing states were under unusual pressure.

It's becoming clear that the politicization of the Justice Department was a key component of the Bush administration's attempt to create a permanent Republican lock on power...eight federal prosecutors fired by Attorney General Alberto Gonzales... for political reasons—some because they wouldn't use their offices to provide electoral help to the G.O.P., and the others probably because they refused to soft-pedal investigations of corrupt Republicans...they wouldn't go along with the Bush administration's politicization of justice. Many other prosecutors decided to protect their jobs or further their careers by doing what the administration wanted them to do: harass Democrats while turning a blind eye to Republican malfeasance."[20] This is exactly what I experienced.

Democrats singled out for prosecution

"Cases abound where Democrats and Democratic elected officials appear to have been singled out for prosecution. . .In Pennsylvania the U.S Attorney General conducted investigations against several Democrats but no Republicans. Puerto Rico's Democratic governor has had his college transcripts subpoenaed and was questioned if he had a hair transplant, where he bought his clothes, and if he had cosmetic surgery. After two and a half years the governor isn't clear what they are investigating."[21]

Georgia Thompson, a state mid-level civil servant employee in Wisconsin, was charged with federal corruption. She was indicted on two felony counts, misapplication of funds, and fraud. She was wrongly convicted of rigging bids on a state contract awarded to a travel agency that contributed to the campaign of her boss, Wisconsin Democratic Governor Jim Doyle. In spite of no evidence that the contract award was improper, no evidence that she benefited from the award, and no evidence that she knew of the donation which was legal, in spite of all this, she was quickly convicted and sentenced to 18 months in prison.

Letter to *Green Bay Press-Gazette*

"...The politicization of federal prosecutors and prosecutions is a serious affront to our Constitution and, as the Georgia Thompson case shows, a serious threat to freedom."[22]

Gonzales denies corruption

Gonzales denied the public corruption charges against Thompson were politically motivated. Thompson served four months in prison before her case was heard by the Circuit Court of Appeals. The Court stated the evidence against her was "beyond thin." In rare move, the Court acquitted her after 26 minutes of oral testimony and ordered her immediate release the same day. The cost to Thompson was enormous: her job, her pension, her life savings, her home, her reputation, and her freedom. Later, the state legislature voted to reimburse Thompson $228,792 in legal expenses but that did not cover her entire cost.

Steven Biskupic's fate

"The U.S. Attorney Steven Biskupic handled the case of Georgia Thompson. Biskupic made a federal case of it, charging Thompson at a time that seemed more politically convenient than legally sound. It seemed to us that Biskupic, a Republican appointee, was trying to embarrass Jim Doyle, a Democratic governor facing re-election.

A federal appeals court confirmed our sense that Biskupic's case was unsound. The judge overturned Thompson's conviction for lack of evidence--acting swiftly and sending a clear signal that Biskupic had blown it. The question that remained was whether Biskupic was corrupt or inept.

Now that the U.S. Justice Department has cleared Biskupic of ethical wrongdoing after a two-year investigation of his machinations regarding Thompson, the issue seems to be settled.

Despite the fact that it appeared he was acting on pressure from former White House political czar Karl Rove, the Justice Department inquiry determined that the U.S. attorney kept politics out of the case.

Then we are left with the fact that Biskupic poured his energies into building a case against an innocent woman--a case that was so unsound that a federal appeals court ordered Thompson's rapid release and went out of its way to note that the U.S. attorney had failed to gather sufficient evidence or develop sufficient arguments to justify his initiative.

In other words: Biskupic was inept.

Ultimately, Biskupic is not responsible for that. The people that put him in the U.S. attorney's position--the Bush White House and its Justice Department--are to blame."[23]

"Mr. Biskupic (in prosecuting Ms. Thompson) may have known that his bosses in Washington expected him to use his position to help Republicans win elections, and then did what they wanted."[24]

You don't have to be an investigator or a lawyer to see the obvious similarity between the Thompson case and mine. Read on.

Illinois – Missouri Study

A research study by Donald Shields and John Cragan, two professors of communication, from Illinois and Missouri, found that U.S. Attorneys investigated seven times as many Democratic officials as Republicans. The professors compiled a database of investigations and/or indictments of candidates and elected officials by U.S. Attorneys since the Bush administration came to power. Of the 375 cases they identified, 10 involved independents, 67 involved Republicans, and 298 involved Democrats. The main source of this partisan tilt was a huge disparity in investigations of local politicians to face Justice Department scrutiny. The study suggests the Department of Justice attacked the Democratic Party at the grassroots level such as Des Moines. This insinuated corruption sapped local Democrats of energy to be leaders of their party and created a suspicion of corruption within their communities. By keeping profiling of local the stories under the radar, such as mine in Des Moines, they were not likely to be viewed nationally.

Bush Administration

The Bush Administration essentially rode into office on a high note. At the time they took over, the country was peaceful. We were in a time of unparalleled economic expansion; financial conditions of the country were improving. Bush essentially stole the presidency from Al Gore after losing the presidential race with the electorate college and later winning it through action of the Supreme Court. He took a wonderful opportunity to unite the country but decided instead to polarize it. Everything became a red versus blue states and us versus them mentality. In the White House, it was politics all the time with Karl Rove assuming his rightful place to the right hand of the devil Dick Cheney. Cheney proved that not only did he not care what the American public thought, but he also was convinced that the executive branch was greater than the sum of all the laws of the country. 9-11 changed this country.

It was when George Bush decided he would use this opportunity to reinvent his lack luster presidency. He assumed his position as Commander-in-Chief by deciding that it was time to turn his energies towards defeating, what he did not understand at the time, Al Qaeda. There was an effort by the country to go after terrorists everywhere.

9/11 and the Patriot Act

The country was mourning 9/11's massive tragedy of the loss of almost 3,000 lives. The travel industry was devastated as individuals cancelled vacations and business trips. An economic disaster hit the country. We were essentially paralyzed. Bush capitalized on this opportunity to erode personal liberties and freedoms by passage of the Patriot Act in the name of going after terrorists. This 1,100-page document was rushed through Congress in the middle of the night. No one had even read the act allowing the federal government unparalleled access into *my* private life, threatening *my* liberties and *my* freedoms. For example, the government used technology to listen to my communications. They tapped into my banking and financial business relationships; they had free access to all of my records. It is illegal for the financial institutions to alert individuals the government was doing this to them. The government, playing Big Brother, began a comprehensive system for data mining, gathering files, and profiling to determine who was or was not at risk. Government agencies went into companies asking to see files of people whose last names contained certain vowels. I was to experience many of these invasions in my privacy over an 18-month period by the government in the effort to destroy me.

DOJ used as political tool

In spite of the fact the DOJ is supposed to be blind to politics, the Bush Administration rebuilt the Department of Justice to use it as a political weapon to go after locally elected officials to create chaos within the Democratic Party. I became one of their targets.

Deace Radio Show

My outspoken liberal views, along with my open sexual orientation, have made me a lightning rod for kooks, bigots, religious far right extremists and conservative talk shows. Some of those characters fit all of these categories.

There were so many weird things occurring along the course leading to my trial. One involved U.S. Attorney Matt Whitaker appearing on the conservative radio talk show, "Deace in the Afternoon Radio Talk Show" hosted by Steve Deace. The show was aired on Friday, March 26, 2007, the week of my highly publicized indictment. After learning I was a topic of conversation between Deace and Whitaker, I paid for a transcript of their dialogue.

Unbelievable!

It was unbelievable to me that a U.S. Attorney would agree to being interviewed in this venue in such a public manner. His behavior was hardly in keeping with the stereotypic dignity and objectivity of a United States Attorney.

The show opened with the pledge by Deace promising ". . .each and every day to fear God." This is not another form of "One nation under God," more like code for "we're very conservative and endowed with a corner on truth."

In addition, four pending cases in which Whitaker was either directly or indirectly involved were mentioned in this interview–CIETC, the Swift Packing Company, his employer U.S. Attorney General Alberto Gonzales, and my case. You'd think Whitaker would have recused himself because of conflict of interest due to pending litigation, the need to protect confidentiality, and/or the necessity of maintaining the dignity of his position. Not Whitaker.

I was baffled to hear Steve Deace refer to gays as "homos" without objection from Whitaker. He made no response—none—to this very derogatory term. It would be like calling African Americans the "N" word. In essence he validated its appropriateness. Deace stated, "Matt (McCoy) is an openly homo, is a guy who left his wife and is now an openly homosexual state senator." Whitaker let the reference to my private life and the word "homo" pass as if it were part of the accepted vernacular among the educated. These comments had absolutely nothing to do with my case which I presume was the reason Whitaker was scheduled to appear. It was unprofessional of Whitaker to allow Deace's comments to go unchallenged.

Deace took another swipe at me before moving on to another topic, "And if nothing else, all the money that uh, he's (McCoy) got pouring in from uh, the gambling and homosexual lobbies he probably will be able to afford an attorney that makes a lot more money than you do to defend him, I'm guessing. We'll come back with more. Stay tuned."[25]

Anyone reading the transcript of the radio show can draw their own conclusions about Whitaker's judgment, intellectual rigor, command of the English language, understanding of the scope of responsibilities of his office, tolerance for those whose values do not mirror his, and his acceptance of human beings who happen to be gay.

Interesting enough, following that show there was an outcry from the public resulting in sponsors leaving the show in droves. Deace also left the station not long after.

Lesson not learned - Whitaker talks about open investigation

Apparently, the criticism following Whitaker talking about open investigations and court cases at the Deace interview was forgotten by Whitaker as he talked about the Mueller hearing during a press conference. This also resulted in widespread criticism and was fodder for late night talk show hosts who jested about his delivery, sweating, and his confusing comments.

MSNBC Transcript: January 28, 2019, The Rachel Maddow Show

Maddow: "Matt Whitaker is a hugely controversial figure as acting attorney general for a whole bunch of different reasons... He was appointed to this job by President Trump. There is every indication the reason President Trump appointed him to this job is because of the long record of public statements criticizing the Mueller investigation...If you are anybody who works at the Justice Department, rule one, you do not talk about open and ongoing investigations."

Narrative from video of Whitaker's press conference

Matthew Whitaker, Acting Attorney General: "You know, I've been fully briefed on the investigation and, you know, I look forward to Director Mueller delivering the final report and I really am not going to talk about an open and ongoing investigation otherwise. But, you know, sort of the statements I made was a private citizen, only with publicly available information. And, you know, I'm comfortable that the decisions that were made are going to be reviewed and, you know, either through the various means we have. But right now, the investigation is I think close to being completed, and I hope that we can get the report from Director Mueller as soon as possible."

Kerri Kupec, DOJ Spokeswoman interrupting: "That's all we have time for today. Thank you so much." (End video)

Maddow: "You can tell Matt Whitaker remembered he's not supposed to opine on the investigation or wax ineloquent on this investigation. You can tell that dawns on him in the middle of the remarks because of the giant soup bowl of hot sweat that breaks out on his head and his face in the middle of him making those remarks when his words start to fail him. And at this point, nobody knows if he said the Mueller investigation is wrapping up...It's also possible he blurted that out in a panic, which honestly looked like he barely strung those words together before the whole thing was called to an end quickly by the Justice Department spokeswoman. Those remarks from the acting attorney general caused a major stir today, honestly, nobody really knows what they might mean."[26]

An anti-gay federal attorney

This gives you a little bit—actually quite a bit—of the history on Whitaker. Clearly anti-gay, he does not mind sitting in a room while the talk show host Steve Deace calls me a "homo." It is my opinion the true color of Whitaker and his anti-gay, anti-democratic, anti-liberal, pro-conservative, pro-religious background showed through. I believe his soul opened to the world that day. Everyone who had any familiarity or closeness to this case recognized that he had targeted me because I was the only openly gay Democratic elected official in the State of Iowa and he was going to see that I paid for it.

Whitaker should step aside from handling McCoy's case

"David Yepsen: 'So we now have the specter of a politically ambitious, evangelical Republican (*Whitaker*) with ties to the religious right going after a gay Democrat (*McCoy*).' Yepsen recommends that Whitaker step aside and let career prosecutors handle the (*McCoy*) case because of the possible conflicts of interest, or even the appearance of a conflict."[27]

Whitaker's case against me built on lies

Whitaker built his entire case against me on lies. Tom Vasquez, Whitaker's star witness and my former business partner turned FBI informant, lied to the grand jury as well as to the FBI. Prosecuting Assistant United States Attorney Mary Luxa lied in writing on a federal form, lied on a Brady violation request, and lied in front of Judge Celeste Bremer. She forgot four times that she approved payment to Vasquez to covertly tape conversations with me. Luxa's illegal behavior had no consequences. Judge James Gritzner aided her lying describing it as an unfortunate lapse of memory. This was an astonishing miscarriage of justice that had the potential of putting me behind bars.

U.S. Attorney General Alberto Gonzales

An additional interesting story emerged. I learned that U.S. Attorney General Alberto Gonzales was in fact a good friend of Whitaker. It seems that when the United States Attorneys got together, this provided the Attorney General an opportunity to spend personal time with Whitaker. This was notably true following Gonzales' resignation as U.S. Attorney General. Gonzales was in Des Moines to give an insignificant speech on child pornography to an obscure by-invitation-only audience. This enabled him to spend part of his final days as Attorney General with his prodigy Matt Whitaker. I'm sure their private times and conversations included my case.

Iowa Senator Tom Harkin's e-mail to Ferguson, May 23, 2007

"I (Tom Harkin) believe Attorney General Alberto Gonzales has repeatedly misled Congress about the firings and he should resign. The Attorney General is the chief law enforcement officer of the Federal government and is responsible for upholding the rule of law. I opposed Gonzales' nomination as Attorney General because his previous record showed he was very involved in the efforts to rewrite and reinterpret our laws governing detention and treatment of detainees in ways that have jeopardized the international reputation of the US for years to come. I also believed he was unlikely to have sufficient independence from the White House. This concern is illustrated perfectly by the firing of the US Attorneys, which originated from and was clearly influenced by the Bush Administration. I believe Attorney General Gonzales should resign, not only due to the US Attorney situation, but to his total failure to properly oversee the FBI's use of the PATRIOT Act powers and his refusal to stop domestic spying by the NSA."[28]

Harkin's e-mail affirms the illegal use of wire-tapping (domestic spying) by the Gonzales Department of Justice.

Reward junkie

I am told Whittaker always tried to impress his teachers and bosses to earn a pat on the head. I was the "shiny apple" on his teacher's desk—another one of those homosexuals who they couldn't beat at the ballot box, couldn't beat at the soap box and decided the only way to beat me was at the jury box.

Whitaker prefers harsher sentencing

"U.S. District Court Judge Robert Pratt said Whitaker's office appealed nine of the sentences he imposed seeking a harsher punishment. 'His office was constantly appealing my sentences to the Court of Appeals,' said Pratt. Who was appointed by Bill Clinton. 'He didn't like my sentences because he thought I was too, I guess, lenient.'"[29]

Whitaker deferred complex decisions to assistants

"Des Moines defense attorney Alfredo Parrish said he believed Whitaker often deferred to the assistant attorneys in his office rather than making complex decisions himself. He said Whitaker had 'good, solid lawyers' working for him in the U.S. attorney's office.

'I want to emphasize that he's very personable, I always got along with him. He always treated me with great respect,' Parrish said.

Parrish, who has represented clients in two cases that Whitaker handled personally, said he was troubled by Whitaker's comments that judges should have a 'biblical view' of the law and found his legal thinking to be 'pretty narrow.'

'He doesn't see what I would call nuance,' Parris said."[30]

Virginia Democratic Senator Mark Warner's appraisal of Whittaker

Senator Mark Warner thought Matt Whitaker's only qualification for acting attorney general was he was against the Mueller Investigation and believed the president was above the law.

90% of federal court cases convicted

"Attorney Matthew Whitaker, a conservative Republican, has denied assertions of political motivation for pursuing the case. McCoy's co-counsel, F. Montgomery Brown, said 90 percent of federal court cases result in a conviction and the swift not guilty verdict (*in McCoy's case*) indicates something was seriously wrong with Whitaker's case."[31]

House Judiciary Committee – my case cited

On February 8, 2010, Matt Whitaker testified before the U.S. House of Representatives Judiciary Committee. Whitaker had been plagued about statements he made concerning the Russia investigation as well as why he has not recused himself from Robert Mueller's investigation. The committee was also interested in learning why he was appointed acting attorney general with his limited qualifications for such a high office.

The Republicans on the committee soft-balled questions to Whitaker. They asked about his accomplishments at the Department of Justice. A Democratic senator in rapid fire shot through Whitaker's past employments, his obtaining huge funding for his non-profit in which he was the only employee, and highlighted a legal case Whitaker had conducted. My case was the one he cited, stating Whitaker had gone after a gay state senator.

"While recapping the oversight hearing, *Deadline: White House* host Nicolle Wallace turned to Frank Figliuzzi, a former FBI assistant director for counter intelligence, to get his take on the acting attorney general's performance…'I'm not kidding when I say I have interviewed terrorists who are more cooperative and respectful than Matt Whitaker was today,' Figliuzzi deadpanned."[32]

Whitaker had to be told during the hearing that senators were not joking and that his humor was unacceptable. The reviews of Whitaker's performance flooded in:

- Combative
- Arrogant

- Contentious
- Confrontational
- Disrespectful
- Political hack
- Stone walling
- Filibuster
- Disdainful
- Dodged questions
- Not forthcoming
- Refused to respond "yes/no" when asked to do so
- Refused to answer questions
- Attempted to set the rules for the hearing
- Had the gall to refer senators to other sources rather than respond to their question
- Speaking to an audience of one (Trump)

I doubt if Whitaker discussed such comments at his celebratory dinner following the hearing held at one of Trump's hotels.

This should concern all of us

Why this should matter to everybody? Because in one short eight-year period, more than 200 years of Constitutional protections, personal liberties and freedoms had been eroded under the watchful eye of George W. Bush and a complacent Congress that lacked the political courage to stand up and tell the Administration they had gone too far. The Bush Administration has proven they not only had contempt for Congress, but had no absolutely no respect for Congress or for the separate and equal branches of government. They packed the courts with their lackeys and packed the United States attorneys' offices with their political hacks. They intended to be above the law. This is what they have done to our country. The assault on our democracy has continued full force under the Trump Administration. That is why this should matter to every American citizen today who cares about their liberties and freedoms.

"We seldom choose the path we are destined to walk.
How we respond to our path is our only choice.
The path I would walk was treacherous and steep.
The truth was my shield and my faith would sustain
me."

Matt McCoy

2

Knock on my door

April 7, 2006--First Friday Breakfast Club

April 7, 2006: A day that will forever haunt me. It was the beginning of unmitigated hell.

I was awake before dawn and dressed to attend the First Friday Breakfast Club, a group of gay and bisexual men who gather monthly at the historic Hoyt Sherman Place built in 1877. Today, the Des Moines Women's Club owns the splendid mansion. It served as the first public art museum in Des Moines.

The Breakfast Club is a unique because it provides gay men the anonymity to come together in a town where everyone knows everyone's business. For years the Breakfast Club met in secrecy for security and to protect member's privacy. The Breakfast Club provides an opportunity for men to connect with the gay community in the larger metro area. Speakers presenting at the club are politicians, community celebrities, and individuals noted for their achievements. The Breakfast Club is a social, educational, supportive organization with a community service component awarding thousands of dollars in scholarships each spring.

My seven-year-old son Jack spends Thursday nights with me. I have made a habit of taking him with me to Breakfast Club prior to dropping him off at his downtown project-based school. He has gotten to know some of the guys who have named him their honorary mascot. A former teacher enjoys giving carefully selected new books to Jack that build upon Jack's interest. It has been a good for Jack because he has met a lot of people, accepting them for whom they are, and learning to be tolerant. This common experience I share with him provides a basis for us to have many discussions about the programs and what it means to be gay.

I am usually up fairly early dressing and gathering up things around the house. I generally wait until the last minute to wake my son, see that he has clean clothes, brushes his teeth and get him out the door.

FBI visit

On this particular morning darkness was beginning to give way to the light of day. I glanced out a window to surprisingly see two stoned-faced young men coming up my sidewalk. I thought, "My gosh, it's way too early for Jehovah Witnesses or Mormons to be out." Actually, I learned later that one of them, Kevin Kohler, is a Mormon. However, on this morning he definitely was not doing missionary work for his church.

Glancing at my watch I wanted to make sure there was time to get Jack up and ready for his day. We still had time to get to the First Friday Breakfast Club, but I needed to move my unannounced visitors on their way. Frankly, it was a bit irritating to be bothered at this early hour. Anyone with kids can identify with my sense of intrusion. Little did I realize what an intrusion I was about to encounter. My life was soon to become a whirlwind.

They knocked. I went to the door, opened it a little bit asking, "What may I do to help you?"

An FBI badge was flashed with the pronouncement they were FBI agents. There were two of them in keeping with their usual procedures of traveling in pairs for interviewing and investigating. They stated they wanted to talk to me about my activities outside the State Legislature. I opened the door and invited them in asking them to have a seat. I sat at a chair with them at my dining room table while my son still slept in his bedroom a short distance away.

They bluntly repeated they were investigating me with respect to my activities outside the Legislature. "Can you tell me about a company called Team Development?"

"Yes, Team Development is my consulting company. I do consulting for companies as well as individuals."

"What did you do besides that outside the Legislature?"

I described what I did as Vice President of Des Moines Downtown Alliance. They abruptly cut me off informing me they were not asking about that.

Specifically, they wanted to know what I was doing with a company called Security Plus, and with its owners Tom Vasquez and Reid Schultz? I explained I had been consulting with them to expand marketing their product Quiet Care.

At that point they cut to the chase, "We are investigating you about issues related to possible bribery, possible extortion, possible violations of the Hobbs Act."

My mind raced seeking order out of the chaos in which I had been plunged. What were they saying? What did they mean? What did they want of me? I wasn't totally certain what the provisions were of the Hobbs Act, but they didn't sound good. I recall thinking, "My God, these guys have made a grave mistake. They got the wrong guy."

So, I told them, "You have made a grave mistake. But, given the nature of what you have just described to me, I feel it would not be appropriate for me to go further without the counsel of my attorney. It would be best for you to leave." I thanked them for their time. Not sure what I was thanking them for or why I said that. Just good up-bringing I guess.

Shocking recording taped surreptitiously

But balding Special FBI Agent Kevin Kohler with his deep-seated eyes wasn't about to be rushed out the door.

"Wait! Before we go we'd like to play a tape for you."

Kohler took out a pretty common looking recorder that he turned on. I remembered hearing some garbled talk that sounded like it had been recorded inside a restaurant. I heard a faint voice. _My_ voice! It was _me_ they had recorded. I laid my head on the table trying to clearly hear. It was that difficult. More difficult still was to comprehend that it was me speaking. That someone had surreptitiously recorded a conversation in which I was involved but totally unaware I was being taped.

It seemed I was having a conversation with Tom Vasquez, my business colleague in Security Plus. Basically, I was telling Tom that if he decided to cut me out of my promised compensation in our consulting agreement, which he and his boss Reid Schultz had made with me, then I would establish my own consulting dealership to compete against them.

I tried to explain to the agents everything I had done in that business was transparent. I was hiding nothing. "Agent Kohler, I can tell you this business was no secret, I disclosed it fully on my Senate disclosure forms that I was involved in business consulting for an ADT company called Security Plus."

Kohler suddenly turned ashen. Facial reactions betrayed his concern. His eyes darted back and forth inside his beady little head.

A visibly worried Kohler was now the one wanting information. Shamelessly he asked, "What forms?"

"In the Senate I am required to file 'Conflict of Interest' forms if I am involved in doing any business with the State. I was involved in selling a good product to the State so I filled out my disclosure forms."

It was abundantly apparent that Kohler had no idea to what I was referring. He had failed to investigate Iowa law. Nor had he been to the Senate to review my disclosure forms. Kohler did not understand the concept of "citizen legislator." State Senators are not highly paid fulltime professional legislators. We are citizen legislators who have to have other employment or personal wealth as we could not live on the low salary of approximately $25,000 paid by the State. And, as a citizen legislator it was totally legal for me to do business with the State.

After playing the tape, Kohler was forthright, "Well that's what we're talking about. We believe that constitutes extortion."

Again, I repeated, "There has been a grave mistake. I'd like to have my attorney."

FBI wants me to snitch on my colleagues

Not satisfied with their dream of getting just me, the bastards told me if I'd give them names of other elected officials engaged in illegal activities, U.S. Attorney Matt Whittaker would look favorable on my situation. So, if I snitched on my Senate colleagues they would cut me a deal. Ignoring the fact that I had no knowledge of what I was supposed to have done illegally, let alone knowledge of anyone else engaging in illegal activities, I would never have played that game. It was re-run McCarthyism. They seemed to be saying give us names or you're in serious trouble.

It was unbelievable, federal authorities asking me to wear a wire to entrap other elected officials. I refused. I had done nothing that federal agents could feel that I could be coerced into doing their dirty work to expand their witch hunt by entrapping my colleagues whose trust I shared. I wasn't about to wear a wire.

I walked these guys to the door fearing my life was about to change. I couldn't possibly have imagined the extent to which it would occur. They left, having taken from me many of my civil liberties.

I suspect Kohler had a busy day covering his ass on this one.

Involvement of Department of Justice

To this day, I sincerely believe if the FBI had done their homework by obtaining my disclosure forms; it would have ended this fiasco. However, for Kohler to drop his investigation at this point would have made him look bad as he had not done the necessary groundwork. Such careless investigating probably would not have earned him praise from his supervisor. I now believe that nothing would have stopped the Department of Justice's wanting to indict a high-profile Democrat in the Southern Judicial District of Iowa. The Democrat they came up with was *me!*

Des Moines

I live in Des Moines. It is in the country's heartland, hardly your stereotypical spot for a federal witch hunt. Those are reserved for metropolitan areas like Chicago or Detroit. Des Moines has a population of 220,000 with a five-county metropolitan area of 635,000. It is a well-run city with little crime. You could describe it as "tranquil." Possessing *real* Midwestern integrity is highly valued. People take pride in being "Iowa Nice." This is one Eagle Scout who had that integrity drummed into me by God-fearing Catholic parents imparting a black/white concept of truth and honesty. It has served me well throughout my life.

My life was about to change

When I finally got them out the door, I grabbed my phone, walked back to my chair and collapsed. My knees were shaking. My face was white. I was bewildered. I was astounded. I was scared. I felt totally violated.

And, I had no clue--why me? I thought, "What in the world could have led these guys to think I was involved in some type of extortion scheme? What in the world would make these guys even want to investigate me?"

And so, began their unending raping of me.

Follow-up to FBI visit
Marc Beltrame

In a situation like this with legal ramifications I do what rational people do, I called my attorney. Marc Beltrame was not only my attorney but he was to be a player in the company the FBI was investigating. Marc was also a close friend.

Marc completed his undergraduate work at The University of Iowa where he was elected president of the student body. Marc later earned his law degree there. He is an ambitious, passionate and impatient guy. He cares deeply about people and probably is loyal to a fault. Marc is an only child who enjoys life and is very close to his parents. Although he had opportunities to work in bigger cities he chose instead to return to his hometown, Des Moines, to work, to make a difference. He volunteers at one of the local high schools as an assistant football coach.

Phone call reveals astonishing news

As soon as the feds departed I phoned Marc.

"Marc, get over here right away!"

Marc's reply was totally void of his usual upbeat manner as he shouted, "Stop whatever you are doing, and you get over *here* right away!"

"Marc, you're not going to believe what has happened to me this morning."

"Matt, you're not going to believe what has happened to me this morning."

Marc was the filer of our "Articles of Incorporation" for our new business, Personal Security Plus, in which he was to be a partner. At exactly the same time I was being visited by the FBI, he was simultaneously being visited by FBI Special Agents Atwood and Decker asking about his role with me in the business I was doing consulting work for Tom Vasquez.

Marc was just as shocked as I was with the FBI's unannounced intrusions. He suggested to the FBI that the afternoon might be a better time for them to visit with him and sent them on their way.

Neither Marc nor I fell for the FBI's shock-and-awe scheme attempting to rattle us into giving poor explanations for what they were seeking. Clearly, they wanted to come into our homes with their witness, probably tape us, probably hoping to hear us say something that would potentially constitute perjury. They may also have been trying to get us to make conflicting or incriminating statements.

Marc rushed to my home. When he arrived, we immediately engaged in an intense discussion trying to ascertain the meaning and implications of what had just taken place. My political and business careers were at stake; his legal license might be in jeopardy. Both our reputations were on the line.

Top lawyer Jerry Crawford contacted immediately

I knew following our discussion and the fact that Beltrame was also visited by the FBI, that my situation was even more terrifying then I originally comprehended—if that was even possible.

I called the person I have always count on for astute counsel. That was Jerry Crawford, a top nationally recognized attorney, who I had known personally for decades. I knew he was an early riser so he would be up. I reached him immediately in Colorado which is on Mountain Time.

Jerry Crawford

Jerry has helped every Democratic presidential nominee succeed in the Iowa Caucus, including John Kerry, Al Gore, Bill Clinton (twice), Michael Dukakis and Hillary Clinton (twice). Crawford established Crawford & Mauro Law Firm in Des Moines, Iowa. He is also known for his investments in the Iowa Energy basketball team, a couple of Kentucky Derby thoroughbred racehorses, and a New York Tony winning play.

For all his accomplishments, he is an understated gentleman. You will not hear him brag about his status or achievements. Crawford is a person who dines with presidents one day and plays golf with his buddies the next. He is highly driven, highly intelligent, and a highly successful well-connected insider.

Crawford has been a life-long friend of my family.

Call to Crawford

Jerry: "What's going on?"

Matt: "You're not going to believe this; I just got visited by federal authorities. I told the agents I needed to speak to my attorney before continuing with them. Jerry, I need to be hooked-up with the best criminal attorney that you can recommend."

Jerry: "There is only one guy who is the type of guy I would recommend. That's Monty Brown. Let me call him to give him your number. He'll call you immediately."

Within the hour Monty called. He was short, directly telling me to meet him in his office at 12:30 p.m.

Taking care of Jack and my employment

Two more important calls needed to be made. I called Jack's mother informing her that I been visited by the FBI. There was some kind of trouble brewing. I was not going to be able to drop Jack off at his school and asked if she would take him. Picking up on the concern in my voice, she immediately came for him. Then I notified my office I would not be in for the day.

Accountant Eric Brewer provides reassurance

Eric Brewer, my accountant, also needed to be brought on-board. He was the author of our business plan for the new business Personal Security Plus. Eric is a bright no non-sense professional. He is sharp on details and ferreting out aspects on financial papers that do not seem right. He cuts immediately to what is important.

I phoned Eric who immediately came to my home. We wanted Eric to go over our business plans, accounting forms, and any other records to make sure everything had been done legally, everything was completed and filed appropriately in a timely manner. Eric assured us it had been. He was just as baffled as we were about what it was that those guys wanted. We were certain the FBI would visit Eric which they later did.

Tom Vasquez

Tom Vasquez and my friendship was complex. It was not social but based on our being in Alcoholics Anonymous (AA) and later working together in business. I had known his family for more than 16 years. I attended church with his mother and father. My former wife worked with Tom's mother at Norwest Bank. Tom and I worked-out together at the YMCA. We met through the AA program. Tom was a long-time member of AA--in and out of the program. By 2007, I had been sober, for more than five years. When I first joined AA, Tom offered to help me with sobriety.

The fact that we were in AA together was publicly announced by Tom during my trial. Tom was always outgoing inserting himself into my life. There is a brotherhood that occurs at AA. We are essentially a group of guys with the same disease that work to keep each other sober. This involves an unspoken bond which everyone usually respects. Tom always was asking me for help which I always provided freely. My perspectives of Tom have been shaped by the AA principle that "no drunk is better than another." I was trained not to judge the character of a person from the past when they were involved in active addiction.

Vasquez's pattern of questionable behavior

I was to learn that Tom had a pattern of questionable behavior:
- abused drugs and alcohol
- had a number of volatile relationships
- had a no-contact order against him by a woman
- had a domestic abuse charge against him
- was a persistent liar

- had recurring difficulties with the law
- lacked remorse for hurting others
- had superficial charm, could be a perfect gentleman
- was unable to make or keep friends
- failed to hold up his end of business agreements
- didn't pay his bills

Tom seemed to leave a path of destruction with those whom he was involved. People who knew Tom described him as:
- "A piece of shit"
- "He's garbage and has been for a long time"
- "Wants to be a big wheel so badly"
- "He has a line"
- "Always has a story, a con artist"
- "He has no work ethic"
- "Always excessive"
- "Has no drive--didn't want to work"

FBI had to know background of their chief witness

The Federal Government's Department of Justice had to be well aware of Tom's questionable background when they selected him to be their collaborator and chief witness against me. Possessing this information raises the question of why the government set out to destroy my entire life based on information provided by the likes of Tom Vasquez? Why? What was their pay-off?

Why didn't I pick up on Vasquez?

Ferguson asked Beltrame why I didn't see Tom for what he was. Beltrame replied, "Matt saw Tom through the prisms of the AA program. Saw him as an alcoholic and drug addict. They bonded through that program. Because of that, I think Matt gave Tom the benefit of the doubt. And frankly, he had no reason to suspect Tom was a bad actor."

As time progressed, I became aware that Tom Vasquez, my business partner in ADT, was my Judas. At this point his deceit of me was far from over. The hypocrite continued to be a paid snitch for the FBI. In retrospect, I can't believe how deeply I was taken in. What followed was rich. I actually counseled my predator, who was bent on destroying my life, to seek legal counsel immediately to protect himself.

Call from Tom Vasquez, ADT business partner

Following the FBI's early morning visit to my home Tom Vasquez called me at 11:19 a.m. Unknown to me, of course, the call was taped for his FBI pals. Transcripts provided by the FBI documented that Tom was calling at the request of the FBI who taped recorded our entire conversation. Feigning innocence, Tom created a scenario that he too had been contacted by the FBI.

Tom: "Do you got a second? I have to tell you something. Are you in a good place where you can talk to me?"

Matt: "I'm at home, yeah."

Tom: "Fuck dude. I just got a fucking call from some guy from the FBI dude."

Matt: "Wanting what?"

Tom: "He's asking me questions, he's like uh, he just introduced himself, and you know, and then he said like uh, do you know, do you know Senator Matt McCoy? And I'm like well, yeah, he's a good friend of mine, he's been a friend of mine for a long time, you know, and he said yeah, well, uh, what kind of business dealings do you have with him and this and that? I said, well, we're looking to set up an ADT dealership and this and that, and you know, he's working on that right now with some folks, you know. And then he said, well what about uh, do you pay him in money? He asked me about paying you money, and this and that. And I was like well, you know, I don't know if I screwed him, well I don't know dude, I mean we're in the process right now of working on a business plan and things for this ADT dealership, I said I don't, I said, you know, I don't, I'll tell you what, I'm gonna have to, um, let you guys, let you go, you know, I'm gonna have to, um, I'm gonna have to talk to an attorney, I said because I'm not gonna talk to you, I said I don't feel uncomfortable talking to you, I want to talk to, I want to talk to somebody else first, you know. I said I don't want to, you know, I'm just in the process of, of you know, working, hopefully, working in the business, you know..."

Matt: "Yeah, well, Tom there's a chance this call is being monitored. Um..."

Tom: "This call? This call right now?"

Matt: "This call, yes."

Tom: "Dude, yeah, so if it, I'm not saying, I'm just telling you the facts dude, I mean…"

Matt: "Yeah, no, I'm just saying, I'm just saying I want you to be very, very careful. Umm, umm. What I want to do is um, I do want to talk to you, I would advise you not to talk to anyone about this, no one. I would also advise you at some point to visit with an attorney about it."

Tom: "I should get my own attorney? Or should I, do you have, do you know an attorney?

Matt: "Well, I would sit tight until I talk to my attorney here and I'll find out. I may have Marc (*Attorney Belterame who was also investing in ADT*) call you back or something. I would just sit tight, umm, and I would not talk to them without representation. You do not have to talk to the FBI without representation, if they don't have a warrant, you don't have to talk to them."

Tom: "What's this all about dude? Seriously, man. I'm up in Ames (*35 miles north of Des Moines*) right now handling some, I'm just, it just scared me to death, dude, I mean I don't, you know…"

Matt: "Stay focused, handle your business. Umm, you know the thing is, you and I had, had, uh, you know we had through my consulting company, we had an agreement. I did business for you and then I, I in turn talked to you about your marketing and story placement and ideas and things like that and anything that you paid me in, income is reportable income which I will report. And um, and I don't see this as an um, I don't see this as a situation where we have any issues but I would just not speak to anyone right now about it, okay?"

Tom: "Okay, like you don't, I mean, you know how things work with us, and with me and you don't think I should talk to my sponsor (*AA sponsor Mitchell*) or anything about it, just keep quiet about it until I talk with you?"

Matt: "I would, yeah, keep quiet, in this case, I think you should just keep quiet because it's a legal issue, I don't want to see you to hurt yourself or anyone else by saying anything. I just think it's better to, I think it's better not to speak to anyone. And um, and then let this thing get, let this thing get sorted out because I think it will. I know it's hard, but I don't want you, I don't want you to worry unnecessarily, so just, just don't, just don't speak to anyone."

Tom: "Well what, I mean, what, what do you know about it, I mean?"

Matt: "I don't know anything about it right now. But I would just tell you that I have a few calls to make, but don't speak to anyone, and um..."

Tom: "I'm just saying, has somebody talked to you, or what? I mean you sound kind of like, you kinda, or are you just relaxed about it, I mean I don't know, I just thought you'd be kind of freaked about it too, you know what I mean? And I don't know..."

Matt: "Well, I mean, I mean Tom, unfortunately, let me just tell you that that um, that you shouldn't speak to anyone about it and you should, you should consult your own attorney. I can't say any more than that other than I would consult an attorney and I would not speak to anyone."

Tom: "Okay."

Matt: "And, if they have any questions make sure your attorney is present."

Tom: "Okay."

Matt: "Okay?"

Tom: "Yeah, cause he gave me a number to call him back, and I you know, I just won't call him back."

Matt: "I would call him back with your attorney."

Tom: "Can you get together this afternoon, what do you want to do?"

Matt: "I can't get together this afternoon, but I'll call you when I can. Okay?"

Tom: "Okay, I'll just sit tight and I'll call a couple, I'll call an attorney, I don't know, do you have anybody in mind that can handle something, I don't know, I don't know what's going on dude, you know what I mean? Is there somebody you can suggest?"

Matt: "Who have you used in the past, or have you used a friend?"

Tom: "Yeah, it's always been a friend. Yeah, it was always somebody...I mean this is the FBI, I mean I don't know does that take a special, somebody specialized in something?"

Matt: "Not really, because your rights are the same whether it's the FBI or anyone else."

Tom: "Uh huh. Okay man. I'm sorry, I'm just all blitzed out about it, you know what I mean. I'm blindsided, I'm up here I get a call, and at first, I mean, I thought I was, I wasn't sure if they were kidding, I mean, I thought it was like, you know, one of your buddies or something calling me, you know just to be like, I don't know, like somebody was messing with you, I mean it just kind of weird."

Matt: "Deep breaths, deep breaths, it's gonna be fine. Take a deep breath."

Tom: "You're a good friend of mine and stuff and that we're about the ADT thing and stuff, when he started talking about money I didn't answer. I just said we're working on a business together you know and that's it."

Matt: "Yeah, and that's all true. And um, let's just, let's just sit tight here."

Tom: "Alright man, well call me if you hear anything or know anything or whatever and I'll make a couple calls here on my way back, cause I you know, I'm in the middle of this and I gotta get my phone book and stuff. And all that."

Matt: "I would make the calls from a landline." (*Knowing that prior to digital cell phones, calls could easily be intercepted.*)

Tom: "From a landline?"

Matt: "Yes."

Tom: "Okay man."

Matt: "Alright, talk to you later."

Tom: "Thanks."

Matt: "Bye."

My asking the likes of Tom to get centered with deep breaths made about as much sense as my having thanked the FBI for having up-ended my life. You don't ask someone who demonstrates an inability to differentiate between right and wrong to "get centered." They simply lack the conscious to care so centering is not possible. Although having the law on my doorsteps was a first for me, I would eventually learn it was nothing new for Tom. If the FBI had been truly after him it would have been just another in a series of his encounters with law enforcement. It was nothing that would cause Tom to worry.

F. Montgomery (Monty) Brown

If you ever need a top defense lawyer go to Monty Brown. His razor-sharp mind, instantaneous responses, through preparedness and strong work ethic makes him a formidable force. He's willing to put in the endless hours necessary to win complex cases. And, he wins.

During my trial he was relentless in questioning, probing, and refusing to let witnesses avoid answering questions. He did not let anyone off the hook. That included me in preparing me for trial. We spend countless hours going over evidence, again-and-again-and-again as well as drilling me on every detail that might possibly come forth in my trail. It was exhausting. But being well-prepared heightened my confidence.

Monty earned his law degree from Drake University. He is currently in new offices in his own law firm, F.M. Brown Law Firm. He handles a wide range of cases--white collar crimes, fraud, drug offenses, homicides, etc.

Jerry Crawford described him as, "an elegant Marlboro Man."

Meeting with Brown

Meeting Brown was absolutely amazing. His office at the time was in Clive, a suburb of 14,000 on the northwest side of Des Moines. The office was in a non-descript long one-story brick building, obviously some type of office building.

Entering, I was hit immediately the pungent smell of stale cigar smoke. Cheap paneling made me wonder if I was in the right place. The "Cook, Brown, & Scott" sign on their door reassured me I was.

The receptionist invited Beltrame and I into Monty's medium size office. It was packed everywhere with documents and papers. A large picture of a fighter pilot's F15 cockpit hung on the wall along with a big stuffed fish. In the corner was an antique boat motor sitting on a stand. A 40-year old cocksure attorney sat behind the desk wearing a golf shirt–the standard pinstriped "uniform" prevalent among lawyers was not for him.

Beltrame later observed: "Boy as first impressions go, I was wondering what the hell we were doing there because here's this guy sitting behind his desk with a big wad of tobacco under his lip. Here's Matt in a pinstripe suit dressed to the nines, a state senator, a respected business leader in the community and here I am working for a member of Congress, also in a pinstripe suit. This guy is treating us like we're drug dealers. He was very gruff."

Monty wasted no time plunging in, "Why are you here?"

"We'd like to know that ourselves." I began telling him about the federal authorities coming to my home and to Marc's. I told him about the FBI's tape with Tom Vasquez's voice.

Brown: "So, it's just you and Tom on the tape?"

"Yeah."

"Well then, Tom was wearing a wire."

"Oh, *really*?"

"Yeah, he must have been or they were taping you from another part of the restaurant. I'm really not sure. I'll have to hear the tape."

"Tom is my friend."

Monty snapped harshly, "Tom Vasquez is <u>NOT</u> your friend. He's trying to put you in prison."

With that, what was happening to me, hit. I couldn't believe it.

Attorney Brown contacts DOJ in Des Moines

While I sat there, Monty called Matt Whitaker's office at the Federal Department of Justice in Des Moines. He spoke with U.S. Attorney Andy Kahl or Mary Luxa.

Brown demanded: "What's going on over there with this McCoy boondoggle?"

FBI: "Your client should come in to talk with us. We have some questions for him to answer."

Monty retorted: "Well, my client is not going to do any talking to anyone and furthermore this thing is a boondoggle. You guys don't know what you're doing and you probably better figure this thing out because I think you've made a big mistake."

FBI: "If that's the case, your client should come in and talk to us."

Monty: "Not going to happen."

Monty's next questions to them almost caused me drop to the floor: "Well are you going to indict him? Arrest him? Put him in jail?"

FBI: "Probably."

Monty: "Is it imminent?"

FBI: "No. The investigation is on-going."

It was obvious that things were extremely serious. Those words and the implication of what could happen to me hit hard. I remember thinking again with utter disbelief that this can't be happening to me. I was in complete denial.

Monty began counseling me on my need to resign from public office. I had no idea why he would make that suggestion. I had done nothing wrong. I knew I was innocent, that this was a big mistake, it wasn't going to happen. I was not making that decision today. Both Monty and his co-counsel Paul Scott provided a bleak overview of what I could expect. They admonished me not to say anything to anyone about this case. We thanked them for their time and we left.

Brown connected the dots

Monty Brown got it. He pulled it all together because he was an objective party. Beltrame and I weren't. It didn't add up. Beltrame, Vasquez and I were in business together. However, the FBI visited only Beltrame and I--not Vasquez. Had I not been so stunned by the FBI's visit I might have put it together. As it was my total focus was on trying to figure out why they were after me and what I had done wrong.

Live life as usual

Monty told me to resume my usual activities. It was one of the most difficult aspects of this whole incident. It was April. The Iowa Senate was still in session. I needed to go back to the Legislature. I needed to be active on the Senate floor, participating in committee meetings, handling bills, collaborating with colleagues, responding to constituents, and at the same time staying very visible in the downtown organization which I was leading. Also, I was taking care of my consulting clients. Plus, being an attentive father to my son and co-parenting with his mother was extremely important to me. My plate was full. On top of all this was added a primary election battle against a conservative Democrat running an anti-gay campaign against me in my first election since coming out as an openly gay official. Actually, at the time I was the only openly gay legislator in the history of Iowa. As such, this also meant I was Iowa's highest ranking openly gay elected official.

You know one of the real struggles that I had with this whole FBI issue was, "Why me? Why were my business practices and I being singled out? Why was I being examined? Who had complained about me? What had activated this investigation?"

"Knowing something about my background, about significant issues in my life, and about my life-changing challenges, may provide insight why I think Gonzales and Whitaker targeted me, a successful elected Democratic official, to take out."

Matt McCoy

3

Not What I Expected:
Bio, Politics, Addiction, Orientation

Biography

Family background

I am the third son of Mary Ann and William McCoy, devout Catholics. They were successful in raising all their children–except me–to be the same. We were a middle-class progressive democratic family living on the south side of Des Moines. The area was a Democratic stronghold with a lot of third generation Italians and Irish. Our large comfortable home was just a few blocks from dad's store, Sellers Hardware. He owned and operated the successful

Sellers for 30 years. It was really a family business because each of my siblings and I took our turn working at the store. My parents instilled the value of hard work through our experiences at Sellers. Both my parents were politically active in progressive, Democratic causes. They were strong advocates for the underdog. Dad continued to be active in politics until his death of Leukemia on March 11, 2015.

I have four siblings all of whom have led successful lives and careers. My oldest brother Mike is co-owner of an insurance company which enables him to pursue his passion as an amateur golfer. Brother Pat is the bond relations manager for the New York City Transit Authority. My sister Molly is a consultant and teacher trainer for Heartland Area Education Agency 11. She was a former teacher, vice principal and the co-author of a mathematics text on instructional strategies for teachers. My other sister, Katie, is a physician assistant in Cedar Rapids.

Formal education

I attended public schools K-2 and 8-9. The remaining grades through high school were in parochial schools. Parochial schools do not encourage a person to deal with their feelings very well and certainly not with their sexual orientation or anything other than "straight". Teachers, counselors, and priests wouldn't have been able to deal with it. The subject of being gay was very, very taboo. This meant many young people felt alone as they struggled in silence fearing ridicule, disapproval or being shunned by friends and family. Although I had very loving and supportive parents, I did not feel in any way I could mention the subject to them. So, I chose not to deal with it. But ignoring it didn't make it go away. It continued to painfully haunt me as I was always on guard afraid someone would find out.

I graduated in 1984 from Dowling Catholic High School in West Des Moines where I was vice president of the student body. In 1988 I graduated from Briar Cliff University, a private Catholic university, in Sioux City, Iowa where I was elected president of the student body. I graduated with a degree in history and political science. It is with some pride that I recall being elected to student council in junior high. That began my political career in which I have never lost an election.

Manly man's work

I spent the summers of my college years working on street construction throughout Des Moines, applying asphalt, tar, and seal coat to streets and roads. This work was enjoyable because it provided me an opportunity to work with manly men and feel my toughness as a macho person who wanted everyone to believe that I was completely straight.

Involvement in politics

High school politics were highlighted by being student coordinator of for all five high schools in Des Moines for Walter Mondale's 1984 campaign for president. I also volunteered in Roxanne Conlin's gubernatorial campaign. Later in college, I found that my passion, my love, was being involved in government. I worked for Joe Biden's Presidential Campaign in Sioux City. When he dropped out of the race I worked for Bruce Babbitt. It was challenging and rewarding.

Elected to office

I was elected to two terms in the Iowa House of Representatives, seven terms in the Iowa Senate, and am currently beginning my first term as an elected Polk County Supervisor. Private employment included Vice President of industry relations at Ruan Transportation, Vice President Downtown Community Alliance, and owner Resource Development Consultants.

Attraction to men

Growing up I knew that something was different about me. I knew that I had feelings that were different than other kids in my class. I knew through my early stages of development I had attractions to both men and women. I knew I was attracted to men in a way that made me feel uncomfortable. I dealt with that by repressing my feelings or desires. But from third grade on I can recall being attracted to both men and women, but preferably men. I felt this was something I could deal with by suppressing it. Attending mass on an almost daily basis, I would pray that this issue would be resolved for me. That I wasn't different. That I only liked women. Prayer didn't resolve it. I remember at certain points along my journey through school I believed I actually was cured of it if there was such a thing as being cured. I wasn't. It was frightening. It was lonely. I was always on guard afraid someone would know my secret.

I realized I had gay inclinations in high school but did not act on them. This was a phase I was going through. It will pass.

Marriage

Jennifer Ann Stitt and I were married on May 29, 1993. I was very much in love with her and believed that she was the answer to my prayers. I was in love with a wonderful woman who loved me in return. And I did truly love her both romantically and as a friend. I honestly felt our love would override any urges I had toward men. We were ecstatically in love. Life was good. Life was going to continue to be good.

Birth of son

Our son Jack McCoy was born May 13, 1999. We had waited six years for him, primarily because we were both busy getting our careers established. In addition, Jenny was obtaining her Masters of Business Administration at Drake University. Our marriage was solid. We were having fun and certainly had a lot in common.

Divorce

But about seven years into our marriage things began to change. One cost of having fast-paced lives where both husband and wife are heavily involved in many areas is that you begin to live separate lives. We began to grow further and further apart. As our marriage began to fall apart, tension replaced love and laughter. These were hurtful days that I hope neither of us ever has to again experience. We separated and eventually divorced.

Politics

Iowa House of Representatives

In 1992 there was an open seat for the Iowa House of Representatives in the district I was raised, and where my parents had spent virtually all of their married life. In fact, my mother was born and raised in the district. All of this was a huge advantage to me as a new comer to the political process. What began as a three or four-way primary slowly whittled down to two candidates. John Brody and I stayed in the race. He had graduated from Lincoln High School which was in the district and had lived on the south side his entire adult life. I was able to defeat him winning around 70% of the vote.

Elected to Iowa House of Representatives

I was only 26 years old when elected to the Iowa House of Representatives which began my political career as an elected official.

I spent two terms in the House of Representatives (1992-1996) and ran for the Iowa Senate in 1996. The Senator that had the seat prior to my announcing had become involved in a public scandal involving a gun, a woman, and drugs. This created a situation where I felt it was time to announce that I was going to run against him. Shortly after my announcement, he dropped out of the race. I ran unopposed in 1996 and went on to serve 22 years in the Senate from 1996-2018.

Re-districting occurred in 2001 that badly carved out my District. I was put in a position where I would have had to run against a colleague. At the same time, there was a new Congressional District formed and I believed that if there was ever a time to run for Congress it was for that open seat in 2002.

Announced run for Congress

I began my quest to run for the United States Congress. I had tremendous support and felt I was backed by a successful career in the Legislature. The timing was perfect. I was in my early 30s. The stars were coming together.

At the same time Congressman Leonard Boswell's district was also re-districted. He now lived in a heavily Republican district. Re-election for him was unlikely. He was our only sitting Democratic Congressman. Boswell decided his home had wheels so he wheeled it to Des Moines to the newly created Third District to pursue the open seat for which I had previously announced.

Throughout the process I continued to stay in the race and had raised close to $100,000. I commissioned a poll to determine what the issues were in the district. I was fully engaged in the race. However, I was encouraged by the Democratic Party to leave the race when Boswell announced he was moving to Des Moines because he was the incumbent. I pointed out, to no avail, the fact that he was not the incumbent, that it was a new district with an open seat.

When I got the poll back I found his name recognition to be very high. During the years that Boswell had served as President of the Iowa Senate and his years in Congress he had developed a very strong name recognition along with a very strong reputation. It would be very difficult and very expensive to defeat him. Congressman Boswell and I met and agreed to shake hands on my withdrawing from the race. I let him know at some point I would still like to run for Congress. He promised to run for only two terms. I would then run at that time. He since changed his mind, decided he liked the United States Congress and ran for his seventh term in 2008. The Congressman lost his bid for re-election that year. Boswell died in 2018.

In 2018, I announced that I would seek a seat on the Polk County Board of Supervisors. I was elected with 82% of the vote against John Mauro who had held the seat for many years.

Alcoholism

The road to alcoholism

I closed-up going into myself as the demons of my being gay surfaced, my drinking increased. Social drinking had always been a part of my life. While attending Dowling Catholic High School it was common for my friends and me to drink on weekends. Social drinking continued in college. Now, as an adult, this was different. I was dealing with issues related to my use of alcohol, primarily consuming too much of it to give me some relief from reality. As my drinking became more frequent and more constant I became a daily heavy drinker.

Every day I would swear this was the day I wouldn't drink. Every night I would find myself buzzed. For whatever reason I was not able to deal with issues I now faced. My marriage was going into a downward spiral. I became very despondent over my home life while at the same time trying to maintain a positive public image. I chose never to drink at public functions. My drinking continued to worsen. It became my refuge. Depression set in. However, I knew I was one of the best actors in town because no one suspected I had a drinking problem. Like most alcoholics, I had fooled myself into believing my close friends and family had no idea I had a drinking problem.

Massive fears about my sexuality and about it becoming public constantly consumed me along with all the baggage it entailed. Attempts to cover them up were becoming futile.

Excessive drinking forces medical attention

People make choices. I had made choices about my drinking. Denial enabled me to continue with the direction my life was going. That is, until I became physically ill as a result of my drinking forcing me to go for a routine physical. My doctor didn't buy my defensive comments about my drinking as he informed me that I had a fatty liver. One of the most common causes of accumulation of fat in the liver is alcoholism. The doctor told me that I might be in the early stages of cirrhosis. Daily drinking had created a health condition that needed to be addressed at once. He was adamant that I stop drinking. I believed I could do it. I promised him I would not drink, that I would deal with this problem and return in a month or two for another test. My usual will-power was strong. Sheer will-power would conquer my out-of-control drinking.

I went home that evening bursting with good intention of not drinking. Right. The next thirty nights were spent drinking. So much for good intentions. So much for inflated will-power. After a month of each day saying this was the day of my last drink, I finally confronted the issue that I was not able to quit without help.

Entered treatment program for alcoholism

Drinking in moderation was my goal. I entered an outpatient alcohol treatment program to learn new behaviors to avoid excessive drinking, to learn to drink in moderation. I planned to continue being a social drinker. I had always described myself as a "social drinker" when in fact I was just the opposite. I was a drunk in denial.

The recovery process was based in part of wanting to get to the truth behind alcoholism. I wanted to understand what caused it. It had been in my family genetics. My father's brothers were alcoholics. Consequently, my father never drank after seeing the pain alcohol caused his family. So, my experience was very limited. I believed that intellectually if I could understand what caused it that I could learn to control it. Of course, that is a fallacy. One of the illusions all drinkers have is that we would learn to control our drinking. That's probably the great obsession that has never been conquered.

I began to understand that my brain was different as a result of my drinking. In fact, I had chemically changed my brain. I had actually changed the appearance of my brain and the way I responded to stimuli. I began to understand this was a genetic disease that I had very little control of as to whether I was going to get it or not get it. One of the most difficult challenges of my life was to get and to stay sober.

I decided I would quit drinking on September 7, 2001! September 11, 2001 the Twin Towers fell and I found myself sitting in a Cedar Rapids bar ordering a steak and a glass of wine which was setting in front of me. I watched, along with our entire population, the catastrophic collapsing of the Towers, the uncontrolled fires, and the stunning human tragedies occurring right before our eyes. Devastating!

I looked at that tempting glass of wine and thought, "It would probably be okay to drink today." As I completed my meal, I realized that I had not touched the wine. I believed that moment, along with my desperate need to be honest about who I am, was my breakthrough that enabled me to overcome my addiction to alcohol. As of 2019, I have had eighteen years sobriety.

Several weeks into my treatment for alcoholism at Mercy Franklin in Des Moines, I began to address some of the issues with how I would live long term with this disease. My counselor advised me to attend an Alcoholics Anonymous (AA) meeting for support. Well, I had *no* interest in being a part of AA. I didn't want anyone to know that I was in treatment. Consequently, all my treatment occurred privately which was an exception that Mercy Franklin made for me. I was adamant that I did not want anyone to know I was an alcoholic. No one was to know I was in treatment.

Alcoholics Anonymous

My counselor insisted that I attend an AA meeting, which I reluctantly did. I chose a meeting near the inner city of Des Moines. It was a late evening meeting. I hoped to sneak in, sit down, and go unnoticed. One of the things about AA is that you never go unnoticed. AA members immediately extended their hands in welcome, introduced themselves, provided their phone numbers along with helpful information and asked about my story. My fear of going was unfounded. They immediately became a supportive and loving community.

I also found that the meetings were full of people just like me. Well not *exactly* like me. We might have had different educational backgrounds, we might have come from different financial circumstances, but we all suffered from the same disease. The similarities in our lives and the stories we shared created a common bond of struggling to overcome our addictions to alcohol and/or drugs. We struggled individually and collectively.

Thus, began my journey to recovery through AA. This has impacted my life in many, many positive ways. I will forever be thankful for the people I met there. They literally changed my life by empowering me to take the disciplined steps required to get back my life. Their support, concern, and information have enabled me to stay sober to this day. Ironically, it was at AA that I met and befriended Tom Vasquez who was to play a formidable role in my life.

Alcoholism tied to sexual orientation

I believe, as I previously stated, an underlying cause of my alcoholism was my inability to openly confront my sexual orientation. Drinking averted the pain of having to come out of the closet. It softened the pain of living a dual life rather than being able to accept who I really was. It became a friend that helped me get through ugly times.

Sexual Orientation

Pete Buttigieg, Mayor South Bend, Indiana, "If me being gay was a choice, it was a choice that was made far, far above my pay grade. And that's the thing I wish the world would understand. That if you got a problem with who I am, your problem is not with me--your quarrel, is with my creator."

"People sometimes view others different from themselves as 'abnormal'. They, of course, are 'normal'. This standard creates broad criteria for what is commonly accepted as 'normal'. Putting others down reflects a sense of insecurity but apparently creates a sense of superiority for them. This is just plain wrong."[33]

Confronting sexual orientation

I recall when I was first able to disclose to my counselor that I was gay. I believed my inability to accept this had an impact on my drinking or vice versa. Alcohol was a means to cover-up my sexual orientation resulting in my drinking more and more. My counselor, T. J. Shay, is a wonderful man. He told me that it was okay to be gay but it wasn't okay to be an alcoholic. I was not going to be able to deal with my alcoholism until I confronted my sexual orientation.

Search for the real me

I searched to understand myself, to find myself, to accept myself as I was born and not to reject the real me. I read widely in the gay press seeking clues as to what it meant to be gay, to match my experiences to those of other openly gay men. I could not transform myself into being the person that met other people's expectations. Accepting who I was became the pivotal point in changing my entire view of the world as well as other's view of me. Once that took place, there was no turning back.

Submerged in the gay culture

To understand what it meant to be gay and understand my own sexual orientation I needed to resolve it once and for all. To do this I submerged myself in a gay culture in San Diego. There I was able to get lost in a new city. Going underground helped to determine what the gay life was really about. I found that it wasn't different than anyone else's life. It just happened to be one that allowed people who live honestly and freely to be themselves among the people they wish to love. There was a real community out there. I learned people cared about each other, very much loved each other, and provided a great deal of support to each other.

One thing I found as I experienced this process was many people have been disowned by or estranged from their families as a result of their decision to come out. Many have never squared things up about their sexual orientation with themselves or with their families. Many a parent has died not really knowing their children. If there was one thing I was determined not to do was to be a mystery to my wife, my son, my parents, my siblings, and to the people in my life that cared about me. The time in San Diego was important. I took several trips there and really got to know who I was.

Conversations with divorced men

During the stressful, painful days of my trying to understand what it meant to be gay, I sought out divorced gay men to hear their stories of becoming aware of their sexual orientation, their marriages and subsequent divorces. A pattern emerged of their not understanding the meaning of their attraction to men, of truly having been in love with their former wives, and having been in deep denial of being bi or gay. Self-loathing was common. Some thought marriage would have changed their attraction to men. Didn't happen. No one blamed their former spouses for their failed marriages. All regretted the agony they had put their wives through. I gained insight into my life through these conversations. The patterns revealed reflected my life.

Rob Borsellino--a man with a big heart and a macro view of life

I recall getting drunk one evening and going into a gay bar in Des Moines. The next day I was completely unable to remember any of the details of my being there. However, a couple of days later, I received a phone call from Rob Borsellino, a columnist for *The Des Moines Register*. Rob informed me that he had received an anonymous letter stating that I was in a gay bar and what I did. They implied that I was gay. The anonymous source thought Rob should explore it and write about it. In essence Rob should "out" me. It was a very hateful letter. Rob didn't read all of it to me but just told me it offended him that somebody would do this. He wanted me to know that I had a helluva enemy out there.

I've always had enemies. I've always been outspoken. When some of these incidents occurred, I think it's important to point out that I was already separated from my wife. I had already made decisions with counselors, with a great deal of therapy, and with a great deal of compassion from my wife, that I would begin to explore gay life to determine what was there. To try to not only understand it but find out if it was what was driving me.

The feeling I had following Rob's call left me stunned with a great deal of anxiety and fear. I was fearful about who would maliciously write such a letter or call a columnist to share that information? The experience was as painful as it was frightening. I would come to learn about my enemies and the length they would go to try to destroy me.

The final time Rob Borsellino called, he told me it had been reported that I was at The Garden, a very large popular gay dance bar. Because of its excellent music many hetero couples also go there. Rob pointed out that you can't expect to keep being gay a secret if you're going out to gay bars. Strange that someone who saw me at The Garden would feel self-righteous or bigoted enough to report it to Rob. Obviously, if they were in a gay bar they were probably gay too. Why would they choose to try to out me in such a public way? This was especially hurtful when I was struggling with whom I was.

I told Rob last time he called that it's okay if he wanted to write about it, it was fine with me. He said he was glad I had come to terms with it but he would not write about it.

I realized that Rob and I had made a connection through the years over lunches together. Though these conversations we had formed an important bond. It was real. Rob was a goodhearted soul who probably knew all along that I was gay and wanted to protect me. At the same time, I think he admired the fact on his last call I told him I'm okay with this, I was prepared to talk about it, and he could certainly write about it. That was quite a transformation for me.

Rob died May 27, 2006, after a long courageous battle with amyotrophic lateral sclerosis (ALS), also known as Lou Gehrig's Disease. His death created a huge loss at *The Des Moines Register*. It was also a loss within our community because despite Rob's tough guy image everybody knew that Borsellino was just a real goodhearted softy on the inside. He would be disgusted with me saying that.

Discrimination against gays prevalent

Yes, there is still tremendous prejudice and discrimination against gays. Subtle things happen that set you apart. It's the failure to get invited to a party that you use to attend. In the office, it's not being invited to going on a hunting trip with the rest of the guys or not being invited to social events where in the past you have always been included.

Someone coming out needs to remember a difficult aspect of living openly is that you never know someone's view about you as you meet them for the first time. If in fact they believe you are a Sodomite, that you have sinned against God and mankind and that you are an evil person. If that is the case, they are going to view and deal with you in a different way.

I don't know another group where subtle discrimination is piled on so heavily with the exception perhaps of undocumented immigrants. But, clearly, if people were doing and saying the types of things about other minorities, for instances Blacks or Asians, or were carrying on the way they were carrying on about gays, it would be considered inappropriate, unprofessional, and unacceptable behavior.

Often times it is what is said, but also what is not said, that brings out fear of potentially being put down or humiliated. Matt Whittaker stated publicly that he made no apologies for being a Christian conservative. He sat in silence while the radio talk show host made comments about my living a despicable life style, my leaving my wife and kid, and that I'm was an openly "homo." His silence is part of that supposedly subtle but strong discrimination against gays.

Sexual orientation--openness

Dialogue at AA meetings begin with stating our name followed by, "I'm an alcoholic." The ritual affirms an unending acknowledgement that we have a problem with alcohol. This public declaration empowers others to come forth. Sharing with others that I'm a recovering alcoholic puts their expectations in perspective (stop pushing booze at me) and frankly saves time having to justify why I don't want a drink.

In being openly gay, I make similar declarations, "I'm gay..." It took a while for me to get to that comfort level, but as in AA, it helps foster tolerance and acceptance of who I am. Perhaps it also empowers others living in the shadows to accept who they really are at least become comfortable with themselves. The message conveyed is that gays and straights have greater commonalities than differences.

As a politician, I found in the long run, it is easier for me to be open with who I am. In being open about my alcoholism and sexuality, I've taken a proactive stance to kill harmful rumors that may fester. My political opponents can't come at me with those aspects of my life because I have already placed them in the public square. People have shared with me that my openness has enabled them to begin to accept themselves rather than continue with their loathing self-hatred. This does not necessarily mean if they are bi or gay they come out of the closet. That is a highly personal decision with a huge impact lasting a lifetime. It does mean they stop beating themselves up for a factor of their birth.

Confronted by Senate Minority Leader and colleagues

That I was gay was shared by me with some of my Senate colleagues who confronted me in the Senate cloak room at the State Capitol. Mike Gronstal, who was Senate Minority Leader at the time asked me point blank what was going on. He had heard a rumor and wondered if it was true. If I was truly gay. I said, "I am, but last time I checked it is not a crime to be gay. Nor was it a requirement that I should in anyway feel like that I cannot serve in the Senate because I was gay."

I could tell he had struggled with that issue. Many of my colleagues asked about my wife, my son, my parents, as they asked what I was going to do with my life. There seemed to be no end to their highly personal invasive questions. In spite of feeling strongly that many of their questions were none of their damned business, I chose to build their support and understanding by responding, "Well I'm going to do the same things I have always done with my life. That is to continue to serve, to continue to be a strong and committed voice for Democratic principles."

This was actually the beginning of a new phase of my life. I recall being miffed that people thought I was going to leave the Senate because I happened to come out. One of the Governor's spokespersons stated that he heard I was gay and asked if was I going to resign? I found that strange because a person's sexual orientation should have no impact on whether they are competent or capable of serving. That would become a fight I was willing to take up as time moved along.

A talk with Governor Vilsack

After visiting individually with dozens of my colleagues in the Senate, I needed to visit with Governor Tom Vilsack who was our Democratic sitting governor. He was the first Democratic governor in thirty years. He was also head of our Party, someone whom I had served with in the Senate, but we were never very close. I made an appointment to see the Governor with the help of my friend Jerry Crawford who was also a friend of Vilsack. The Governor invited me into his office. I recall the Governor sitting behind his desk. I was sitting next to the Governor who asked, "What is it that you have come to talk about today?"

I explained to him I had been on a journey. I was discovering things about myself. I am battling alcoholism and wanted to share with him that I was gay. You know that was a frightening, difficult and understandably humiliating conversation. At the same time Governor Vilsack needed to know that folks were going to be coming to him saying, "What's up with McCoy? What's up with his Senate seat? What's happening? What's he going to do? What are you going to do about him?" He needed to hear it directly from me, to have first-hand information. I needed to have the courage to have a direct face-to-face dialogue with him.

I wanted this Governor to be brought in. I wanted him to be part of my support system. To his credit, he took the news very well. I found him to be very compassionate, very understanding, and very supportive of me. Vilsack was also Catholic. Because of this, I shared with him that I was not feeling much support from the Church. This was especially in light of some of the outrageous things the Church was distributing about homosexuality. I told him that I probably would not be remaining a Catholic. The Governor encouraged me to go where I could find a spiritual home. I found him to be extremely empathetic in his approach to me.

My last opportunity to interact with Governor Vilsack was during his final State of the State Address. As he prepared to leave his office, I asked to escort him to the House and to the podium where he would deliver his address. He agreed. As symbols for the day, I wore a pink tie and had a pink handkerchief folded in the triangle symbol in my suit breast pocket. The pink triangle is the recognized symbol for gay rights. It was used by the Nazis in concentration camps to label gays for execution. This negative symbol has been converted into a positive symbol proudly worn. I wanted this Governor to know that I appreciated him and the support he provided me. It was a very symbolic experience.

My story changed minds and votes—
Democrats opposed to banning same-sex marriage

"In Spring 2004, Iowa Senators were keenly aware Republicans were pushing a debate on a Constitutional Amendment that marriage was only between a man and a woman, thus banning same-sex marriage.

In the Democratic caucus, McCoy spoke about his life and his opposition to the resolution. Most if not all, of them already knew he was ready to acknowledge his sexual orientation. If people asked, he would acknowledge it without going any further. The last thing he wanted was to be known as Iowa's 'gay' legislator.

But as McCoy addressed the caucus, he noticed a wave of sympathetic emotion welling up among his colleagues. The story of his battle with alcoholism and the slow and painful struggle to accept his sexual orientation had struck a chord with almost everyone."[34]

Publicly outed on floor of the Iowa Senate

Although McCoy was still not out publicly, his colleagues felt his being open with them about his sexuality was the significant turning point for the caucus. They had a gay member of their group whom they were going to support.

A lot of things had changed since 1998 when I voted in the Senate for a constitutional amendment to restrict marriage to a man and a woman. I had experienced major changes in my personal life. Our culture was beginning to change as well. I continue to regret that vote.

McCoy would not only vote his conscience this time but would also voice his opposition to the proposal from the senate floor, calling it 'meaningless, mean-spirited, discriminatory legislation.'

In response, (Senator) Veenstra directly addressed McCoy and alluded openly to his homosexuality. Until then, the subject hadn't come up in a public debate. News reports would declare that Veenstra had outed McCoy on the senate floor.[35] McCoy felt insulted but did not respond.

Vote for the Amendment failed 24-25.

April 7, 2009

Ferguson interviewed Ken Veenstra, at the Capitol during a visit by the former state senator on April 7, 2009.

Ferguson: "Did you out McCoy on the floor of the senate?"

Veenstra: "Not entirely accurate. McCoy's sexual orientation had become obvious in '04 when a constitutional amendment was introduced stating that marriage was between one man and one woman. This occurred after McCoy had announced his sexual preference–gay life

When that became public, I raised awareness in this body (Senate), particularly for those of us wanting to stand against gay marriage. Later on, when time for me to run for re-election in the mid-term elections gay marriage became a campaign issue which lost the primary election for me."

Ferguson: "You were openly vocal against gay marriage in Iowa?"

Veenstra: "Yes, it violated the Constitution and violated moral law that governs my behavior. That law is expressed in the Bible that obviously didn't approve of gays. McCoy and I are born and given life by our Creator. We are both children of God. No difference. In the process of living, some of us choose a different life style. He wasn't always that way (gay). At some point he chose that life style. I didn't agree. My respect for him as a child of God did not diminish even though I didn't approve, I spent time in prayer for him and others that God can actually change their view about this issue. McCoy made life choice. I think those choices are wrong–morally and socially."

Ferguson found Veenstra to be pleasant, self-righteous, rigid in his religious beliefs, and programmed on his opposition to gays. Had they not talked about his beliefs or McCoy, he would have come off like a nice guy with a warm smile. He sincerely believed he did not out McCoy.

I am the same guy I was before I came out

After coming out I almost had to assure people that I was the same guy that I was before announcing I was gay. For some, there was an unspoken question about my identity in terms of who I now represented in the Legislature. Was I a gay senator representing the gay community or was I a senator who happened to be gay representing all of my constituents? It was obvious to all those who followed my career that I was dedicated to my constituents without regard to age, gender, color, orientation, faith, political party, or origin. I have continued to represent and be supported by all my constituents.

In his doctoral dissertation, which incidentally I was the focus of his research, Daniel Hoffman-Zinnel dealt with this question: "There are different types of candidates within this (gay) community. Two of these types include gay candidates and candidates who happen to be gay. Gay candidates run to represent the prominent or significant gay community within their constituency. These candidates run on a platform with gay rights and equality at the forefront of their purpose for running. Candidates who happen to be gay are individuals running in a community that may not predominantly or significantly gay but rather a constituency of the general population that includes gay constituents. These candidates run on a platform that is more general in terms to benefit the whole community, although they can be and often are passionate about gay rights and equality. (Yeager, 1999)."[36]

*"A democracy runs on truth and truth is the basis
of what unites us."*
                                    Rep. Jamie Raskin, Maryland[37]

4

What Happened

Recruited by Vasquez

I was approached in June 2005 by a friend to sell a home monitoring system. Tom Vasquez, as I previously stated, worked out with me at the YMCA and was also a "brother" in Alcoholics Anonymous. He needed business expertise for Security Plus, a company he claimed he owned. This was one of his many lies. The pathological liar didn't own that company, or much of anything else. He was a sales manager in a two to three-person operation run out of his boss' garage. I happened to have a consulting company with the expertise he was seeking.

On July 15, 2005, Tom invited me to meet at Temple Starbucks where he demonstrated the product Quiet Care. This home monitoring system was a high-tech way to record an elderly person's movements within their home. The computer records this data on a monitor located in the home of someone related to the elderly person. It enables family members to know when their loved one is awake, if the person is taking their mediation, and if they are tending to personal hygiene. It's a double win. The elderly remain in their homes longer, and family members have peace of mind that they are safe.

The technology and concept were impressive. As luck would have it, that evening I was watching CBS's 'Eye on America.'[38] To my amazement, they featured the Quiet Care home monitoring system. Sold!

The next morning, I phoned Tom accepting his offer to work for him in his company Security Plus and telling him, "I will help you take this product to the moon."

Save taxpayers money

One area that I envisioned marketing Quiet Care was to the State of Iowa. At that time, the average monthly cost of having an individual in a nursing home was approximately $2,500. I thought by extending the time older people can live independently, we could save tax payers up to $30,000 per year per unit sold.

State disclosure forms completed

Therefore, to do business with the State I filled out all the personal business disclosure statements required by the State and Iowa Senate for full transparency. In addition, I took the extra but not required step of checking with the Senate ethics person to ensure everything I was doing was open and above board. It is not illegal for me as an elected official to do business with the State as long as I reported my involvement.

Reid Schultz, Tom's boss, applied to the Iowa Department of Human Services (DHS) to become a vendor under the Personal Emergency Response System. He applied as Security Plus of Des Moines. However, he failed to complete the application and did not finish enrollment. They needed my business acumen.

Meetings with the Department of Human Services

The Governor had expressed a desire to keep older citizens in their homes as long as possible. To move his agenda and this product forward I arranged a meeting in the summer of 2005 with Kevin Concannon, Director Iowa Department of Health & Human

Services, for Tom and I to discuss Quiet Care. The meeting was short with Concannon sending us to meet with Gene Gessow, Iowa Medicaid 63 Director, Department of Human Services. So, on August 24, 2005 Tom, and Tom's boss Reid Schultz and I met with Gessow. It was embarrassing. Tom and Reid did not have their act together. They were told by Gene that without providing additional information the State would not consider their proposal

When this meeting with State officials collapsed, it had to be unquestionably clear to Tom and Reid that we were going to have to work to get this sale. It had to be evident to them my position as a State Senator carried no weight in negotiating our business agreement. We had to win the sale.

I lacked authority to influence marketing with State

It also had to be obvious that I did not have the authority or influence to give or withdraw State support for our product. Therefore, Tom later could not state with any integrity that he felt threatened by me having the State terminate our agreement with Security Plus if he did not fulfill his promised commission to me. All of this would become crucial during my trial for one count of attempted extortion.

I had my work cut out for me to get those guys together enough to make a solid case to the State. I obtained and formatted the information Gessow had requested for the State. I complied with my part of my oral contract with Tom by providing extensive, time-gobbling services. These included pulling details together for sales, formatting sales presentations, training them on effective sales presentations, briefing them on sales strategies for our meeting with the State, obtaining and preparing media interviews, and advising them on an ADT (corporate manufacturer of Quiet Care) National Convention presentation on our niche selling to the State of Iowa.

On September 2, 2005, I presented the materials I had put together to Medicaid. Tom participated claiming Medicaid as his own work. I'm not certain even today he would give me credit for bailing him out of that one.

Vasquez agrees to my commission

Tom was more than pleased that I was working with him. But, we still had not discussed my compensation. With the amount of work involved, he had to recognize I couldn't just donate my time. When asked by Tom what my commission would be on each unit sold, I replied $100.00. It was my understanding that Tom's commission was approximately $400.00 - $500.00 per unit depending on the model. Tom would be paying me from his commission. The manner in which Tom paid my agreed upon commission, and the manner in which I accepted it, does not reflect a man under duress. In paying me, he once commented, "You earned it."

Tom represented to me that Reid Schultz got a small cut from the commissions. He led me to believe that ADT Quiet Care System Company was his and would also become mine. He thought a commission for me of $100 per unit sold through the State would be fair. He should think it was fair, it was he who had originally thrown out that figure. I later learned that Tom had also offered other potential sales people $100 per unit sold commission. I also learned that Schultz owned the company, not Tom, and that Schultz was unaware of, and had not approved, my commission or involvement.

I trusted Tom to pay me what I was owed. I never requested documentation verifying the number of units sold, thereby making sure someone was not skimming off the top what was due me. I simply accepted his word.

Paying someone in cash for services or product rendered came up during the trial. It was a pivotal topic in jury deliberation. In trial, Vasquez accused me of greedily saying "Cash is King!" My attorney Monty Brown challenged Vasquez reminding him that in reality, it was he who used the phrase.

"Cash" is a red flag in theory. Tom's first payment to me for my commission was paid in cash. I did not request Tom pay me in cash. Actually, cash payments are not synonymous with illegal behavior. Cash is legal tender in the United States. We cannot refuse to accept cash payments. Once again, we were talking about small amounts of money totaling $1,800 over several months. Frankly, I did not look to see the form of the payments when I received them as they were in envelopes. Tom made the decision on how he would pay me–cash or check, when he paid me, and how much he paid me. I allowed Tom to work within his financial constraints. People in poverty or with limited financial resources seldom have checking accounts and therefore make payments in cash. Tom had limited financial resources.

Once, as Tom paid my commission, he complained he needed money. I immediately returned the money he had given me stating, "Well Tom, you keep this. I don't need it." Tom took back $80. This small amount suggested he was having a lot of financial difficulties. If Tom's payments of commission to me were bribes, as was later implied, I would not have told him to keep the money due me. This does, however, reflect my feeling that we had a trusting, caring, supportive relationship.

In speaking of money, Tom could not have felt he was being extorted when under the new corporation we were forming he asked that he be paid $80,000 annually!

KCCI clip on Quiet Care

Arrangements were made by me with the local television news station KCCI to present a clip on our product Quiet Care. All aspects of our appearance had been orchestrated by me--pitching the story to KCCI, completing a media outline for Tom, scheduling the person whom we were to film. The fact that Quiet Care had been on CBS's "Eye on America" helped move this along with its affiliate station KCCI. The clip aired on September 28, 2005. A wonderful friend of mine, Marguerite Avant, invited us into her home to share her reliance on Quiet Care. KCCI's Stacey Horst innocently led into the clip, identifying me in my role as a State Senator, "An Iowa Senator is planning to push for a new program to help keep seniors in their homes and save the State money in Medicaid costs." In fact, KCCI titled the segment, "Senator Plans to Push Elderly Home Monitor System."

Later, Cynthia Fodor, who interviewed Avant, went on to say, "State Senator Matt McCoy says this can give peace of mind to children and save the State money." My response that followed naturally elaborated on Fodor's observation, "The average cost on a monthly basis of having an individual in a nursing home is approximately $2,500. If we can even prevent one senior from entering a nursing home by a year or two years we can save tax payers up to $30,000 per year."[39]

Words that seemed so innocent at the time later came back to be used against me. The FBI used this clip as a key factor in manufacturing charges against me. This was "evidence" of their claim that because I was referred to as "Senator" in that television clip I was using my office as a State Senator for personal gain. Cynthia Fodor is a friend of mine. In setting up this program, I explained to her Tom Vasquez was a client of mine, I was coming to her in my capacity as his consultant. Obviously, she knew I was a State Senator. I did not bring it up.

People often called me "Senator" even when I was acting as a private citizen conducting business. During my trial newspaper clippings were introduced by my attorney Monty Brown as evidence to show that in performing my role as Vice President of the Des Moines Downtown Alliance, the media often incorrectly used my title "Senator." That I happened to be a Senator had nothing to do with what I was doing for Downtown Alliance, which was talking about landscaping. This occurred time and time again, but this time it was problematic because the FBI *wanted* it to be a problem.

Three days later Avant and Vasquez were in an article in *The Des Moines Register* that I had arranged. However, this time I was not mentioned.

Vasquez complains about Reid, wants new company

In late August 2005 Tom told me that he wanted to leave his boss Reid Schultz. He wanted me to start an ADT dealership with him. Tom told me that he was unhappy with the way he was being treated by Reid. His list of grievances against Reid was long. According to Tom, Reid wouldn't invest in advertising, deal with his son who came to work drunk and who screwed things up when he did bother to show-up, pay him on time, cultivate a relationship with new vendors, establish relationships with new home builders, rent office space, invest in technology, invest in the camera equipment side of the business, or set up a kiosk at the mall.

Investigate forming my own company

Following the principles of our free enterprise system, I begin in September 2005 to investigate forming my own company. The product was good. Good enough that I told my parents I wanted them to install one if ever needed.

The more I learned about the product and other products offered by the manufacturer the more I realized Schultz and Vasquez had limited marketing vision. Working with them was a dead-end operation. Their inability to maximize opportunities was apparent. Envisioning its potential was exciting--a full house monitoring system that included entertainment systems along with home security. Housing contractors would install this total communication package during the construction of new homes. Going national would generate a generous income.

Consequently, I began dialoguing with the parent company, ADT Corporate. We signed a "Confidentiality Agreement" binding both of us to silence as far as my developing my own business. Ideas shared with them for the new company were thus protected. It also gave distance from Schultz and Vasquez. The agreement was signed on October 12, 2005. ADT violated it on October 25 by informing Schultz and Vasquez about my plans to compete against them.

Vasquez's complaint to Des Moines detective begins my nightmare

This is important as it gave Tom the information that I was forming a competing company in which he most likely would not be a player. It provided the motivation for Tom's betrayal of me. As I moved forward to formalizing a competing business, Tom feared being iced out. He feared he would lose income, connections, and business smarts. Fear can be the breeding ground for discontent. It can create panic and possibly lead to desperate acts. For some unexplainable reason, Tom inaccurately thought I would--that I actually could--cancel his business with the State. His fear of not being part of the new company caused him to gripe to his AA sponsor, Des Moines Police Detective Lieutenant Terry Mitchell. Mitchell, in his ignorance of Iowa law pertaining to citizen legislators, declared I was breaking the law by selling to the State. It seemed logical that fear of being cut out of the new company; fear of competition along with economic uncertainty had driven Tom to make frivolous and false statements to levy charges against me. Connecting the dots provides the sorry rationale for

Tom's behavior. Mitchell immediately went to an FBI friend who connected Tom with the FBI. Within 24 hours Tom began to covertly tape record my conversations with him. I have wondered if Tom ever thought this thing could snow ball so fast and become too large for him to handle.

In reality, Tom and Reid had more to worry about with their corporate headquarters then they did about me. On October 25, ADT unethically shared with me they were unhappy with Reid. Lack of sales resulted in his being in breach of their distributorship agreement, meaning ADT could terminate that agreement at any time.

At this time, I still had not determined if Tom would be a part of the new business venture. I e-mailed Tom regarding a marketing plan I had asked him to develop. He gave it to me. I told him, "This is well done and I think it reflects the type of aggressive marketing that we will use to penetrate and dominate this market. Give me a call if you don't understand what I am asking for. Good work and thanks for your great ideas. There was not a bad idea in the entire bunch." Tom had given me a list of ideas without specific details. I was praising him and at the same time asking him to flush out the details.

Our accountant, Eric Brewer, e-mailed Tom in early November regarding that same marketing plan, "Expand on some of your marketing techniques. Try and refine some criteria on the geographies. Explain the benefits we offer. Try and incorporate the idea of obtaining a 'quality sale'. On some of the techniques, try and identify costs."

Questioning Vasquez's value to new business

Tom wanted desperately to be a player in the new business. So puffed up was he with his own self-importance, that he wanted to be put on a salary of $80 – $90,000 per year! My business partner Marc Beltrame freely expressed reservations about Tom. We were in a *Catch-22*. We were questioning Tom's value to the business as well as his integrity. At the same time, he had been involved since the conception of our plans. Tom also knew the business, or so he claimed. How Tom could feel he was being extorted when under the new corporation we were forming he asked not only to be an important part of the management team, but to be paid $80,000 annually? Nice work if you can get it.

When exploration of our business began it was ascertained this dealership had a low capital entry cost and potential for a generous upside. The "Articles of Incorporation of Personal Security Plus, Inc." was filed with the State for our new corporation. Ironically, Tom had come up with the name for the business.

Corporate ADT apparently were not among Tom's fans. In a mid-November we were to meet with them regarding obtaining a dealership. They directed us, "Don't bring Tom."

Commission paid hardly offset my cost

Not all was lost for Tom with Reid's business Security Plus. The Department of Human Services had approved them selling to the State. Because of this, 18 units were sold to customers with Medicaid bearing the cost. My agreed upon commission for these sales was $100 per unit, or $1,800. This unquestionably heightened Tom's worry of being dumped mistakenly thinking he would lose this venue.

Remember, all the fuss with the FBI was over my having received $1,800 compensation for my work? The good guys labeled it "bribery." Interestingly enough, on December 9, I cut a check from my Team Development account for $1,518.75 to Eric Brewer for accounting work on our new business, Personal Security Plus.

During this period, Tom continued dialogue with me on formalizing our business relationship into a corporation according to our oral agreement. Amazingly, this conversation continued through April 2006 when the FBI came knocking. Tom and I met regularly for coffee and sometimes meals. I always picked up the tab. Tom never paid for anything while I was around--hardly the behavior of a guy who believed I was extorting him.

Taping

FBI's secret taping of 12 hours of conversation between Tom and me carried with it the risk of back-firing. And, it did. It was used extensively by my lawyers to invalidate their charge of attempted extortion. It revealed a lot of about Tom's character. Tom had become a paid "rat," as he was referred to with distain by his AA brothers who taunted him with offers of cheese. That alone said a lot about his character.

Following an AA meeting, Tom taped a conversation with an unidentified member. Although we had a pretty good idea of whom Tom was talking to, we couldn't prove it. Transcript of that conversation on Sunday, December 4, 2006 were provided to my legal team by the FBI but not used by then during my trial. I have wondered if Tom had his tape recorder running during our AA meeting where trust and confidentiality are basic to its success.

On Tuesday, December 6, 2006 Tom and I met in the dining room of the Savery Hotel. Tom wore FBI's wire. Schultz was to have joined us for this meeting but was a no-show. I had yet to meet the man. It was the comments that I made at this meeting, such as "I will compete against you," that the FBI construed to be alleged threats. I told Tom if they didn't honor the commitment that he and Schultz had made to me regarding my commission, I would walk away and compete against Schultz with my own company. From my perspective, this was merely a heated business disagreement.

12 long hours of tapes

There were twelve hours of my conversations with Tom that he had secretly taped recorded. I understand this was done by my trusted colleague wearing a wire. Our conversations were also taped in a coffee house by someone sitting at an adjacent table. The full twelve hours must be listened to in order to gain an accurate perception of our relationship. Conclusions cannot be accurately drawn from brief snippets in a long documentary. Those were merely snapshots of instants in time. It was unfair of the Federal Government to take a few minutes out of twelve hours of tape to support their preconceived conclusions. Listeners need to be mindful that Tom was baiting me, setting me up, and entrapping me. Listeners need to ask, "Did Tom sound fearful?" "Were Tom's questions trying to get me to respond in a way not consistent with thoughtful dialogue?" "Did Tom clearly accuse me of extortion or implied extortion?" "Does it sound as if Tom and I were trusted colleagues?" "Was Tom a paid informant for the FBI?"

I tend to use colorful speech, saying things sometimes just for the fun of hearing myself talk. Actions, however, do not necessarily follow. In the case of my conversations with Tom there have been absolutely no follow through on anything I may have said. Although I have an excellent vocabulary, I use colorful language which can be earthy, vulgar, and even profane.

Meeting with Reid Schultz

I finally got together again with Tom's boss Reid Schultz at a meeting with he and Tom. The meeting took place in my office on Wednesday, December 21, 2005. Unknown to me, the meeting was secretly taped by Vasquez who was wearing a wire. The FBI provided my attorney Monty Brown a copy of the transcript of that taping though Brown's request for Discovery Material.

Schultz said that it was his understanding is that for every Quiet Care they installed, I would be given (*earn*) a hundred dollars.

I reminded Schultz that Vasquez had said he questioned what I brought to the table. I told them directly that because we will be dealing with the State, I will register my conflict of interest with the State in case anything pertaining to this project would come up through the Appropriations Committee of which I'm co-chair.

As our conversation continues, Vasquez asked, "What, do you want to continue and just do the hundred dollars a deal or do you want to make a, you know, some type of, of agreement, do you know what I'm saying?"

McCoy: "No. Uh, Yeah, I, I, I mean, that was our...that was my understanding."

Schultz: "Now what, what'll happen now, you know if, if I don't agree to pay a hundred dollars a deal?"

McCoy: "Nothing."

I brought forth in the conversation that they are aware that I have talked with Corporate about setting up my own company and sale the product, or a newer version of it, or a similar product from another vendor. Schultz expressed concern he might lose business if I set up my own company. I told him that I couldn't speak to that. I told Schultz that maybe I should have talked directly with him instead of Tom about my involvement in the business. I told Schultz, "I would respectfully allow this verbal agreement that I have with Tom to evaporate and you guys can do what you need to do and that I'll do what I need to do."

Schultz continued to discuss profit margins and what he could pay me but could not set a fee until he talked with his accountant.

I told them both, "I think it'd be easier if we just both operate our own businesses and not have any hard feelings. That's the last thing I want. If you don't want me in your business then I'm out. I will not sit here and extort. I will not sit here in any way put myself in a position where I feel like I'm compromised or I'm compromising you. And so, it would be easier for me to sever the relationship and not accept any compensation and wish you well and let me go do what I need to do in the way of business. And it's not personal, it's just business. I'm feeling very uncomfortable with the position I'm in right now. I feel like I've, been duped. Things happen and you move on."

I told them that I don't want to feel like they feel if they don't do this now that I'm going to go get the (State's) business. I told them, "There's no assurance of that Reid...nor am I threatening that we either have a relationship going forward or we don't have a relationship going forward. Either way it doesn't matter to me. Look, no matter what happens here, I say we all shake hands when we're done and we part as friends. We just shake hands and you owe me nothing."

Later, in reading through the transcript on Tom's tape, I became aware of how often Vasquez introduced money into the conversation. All of this was on tape in the possession of the FBI. In retrospect, I realize the tone of this conversation was different. I had come to terms with what was taking place. I was comfortable with it. I no longer wanted to be a part of their business. I was being secretly taped--brutally taped--by Tom and I was still loyal to my betrayer. The FBI had to realize I was calm through all this--a gentleman. I did not take Tom's bait, I made no threats, I told them I was going to file all necessary documents with the State, and I told them we could go our separate ways and remain friends. This should have ended the FBI's and Whitaker's relentless assault on me.

ADT Corporate, the parent company of the product Quiet Care, had talked with me about forming another company. It was my understanding ADT violated our Confidentiality Agreement. I told

Schultz and Vasquez that I was considering opening an ADT franchise dealership which would compete with them. I informed them I would compete against them and beat them fair and square and may the best man win. I escorted them out of my office. Before doing so I hugged Tom. As in the "Godfather," the message was clear: "Goodbye, we are done!" Our business relationship was dissolved. As Tom left he said he would call me.

Vasquez plays both sides of our business against each other

After Reid Schultz left my office, Tom returned immediately saying, "...Schultz has a check for you, dude. Let us give you the five hundred dollars." I responded, "No. I'm not going to take it."

I essentially told Tom I thought Reid was a jerk. I'd never met such a guy in all my life. He was clearly somebody who didn't recognize those who were helping him. I didn't want to be part of being associated with a person like that. My anger was real. Not anger with Tom, but angry because after weeks of productive work that got results this guy questioned what I brought to the table. A reality check would have revealed Reid would not have been able to have advanced his product had I not helped him with his sales strategies and marketing. Tom agreed and said he couldn't believe what an idiot Reid was. Reid was not supposed to have questioned my contributions to the business. Tom was supposed to come back in and resolve this issue about my promised commission. Tom was completely flabbergasted by it. He claimed to be so mad at Reid that he was not even going to speak to him when they left the building. Tom presented Reid as our common problem.

Not pleased with Vasquez

I was very angry that I was getting mistreated, deceived, and cheated. I was angry with Tom for not having kept Reid fully informed on all the work I had done. Tom called the following day telling me Reid had screwed-up. I would never have to deal with Reid again. Tom told me that his agreement and contract with me for my commission would be honored per our agreement. In spite of all of this being recorded by the FBI, they still pursued me hunting for a crime to hang on me.

My phone call to Vasquez recorded by FBI

Later that day, I phoned Tom at 2:41 p.m., leaving a message which the FBI recorded and later thoughtfully transcribed:

Matt: "Hey Tom, Matt calling here, I just wanted to uh, I wanted to touch base with you again I uh, I didn't feel like I left you on a very good note and I felt bad about that, but that guy (Schultz) just pissed me off so bad, that I couldn't stomach it another second so, anyway, um, I've done business with a lot of people in my time but never one that was such a fuckin piece of shit. Anyway, give me a buzz. Talk with you later, bye."

Vasquez could not be trusted

In retrospect, it was evident that Tom could not be trusted. He had lied to me about his owning the business, he badmouthed his business partner, he was ready to dump his business partner, he apparently had not been supportive of me to Reid, and he had tried to terminate our original contract.

Although I did not accept their $500 check the first time it was offered, I did accept it on December 29, 2005 when I met privately with Tom at Winston's, an eatery on the Des Moines skywalk. The check was made payable to Team Development. Later I learned the FBI had provided my double-dealing friend with the money to pay my commission. Tom was wired for our conversation. The FBI with all their state-of-the-art technology was unsuccessful in attempting to video tape our meeting. They had better luck on January 16, 2006 when they videotaped us having coffee at Java Joes Coffee House. Tom, of course, wired up for that meeting too.

Required forms filed with Iowa Senate
Statement of Economic Interest

I filed the required disclosure form with Iowa Senate Statement of Economic Interest on January 18, 2006 listing myself as a consultant on security issues. The name of my consulting firm, Team Development, was cited.

Tom and I continued to have numerous meetings through February and March, each of which he was paid by the FBI to tape record. I wasn't Tom's only lunch partner. On February 8 he met with the FBI at Drake Diner to discuss deceptions laid on me. I have no doubt as to who got stuck with the lunch tab.

Forms filed with Iowa Ethics and Campaign Finance Disclosure Board

Still under the false impression that we were moving forward in good faith in our business, on February 28, 2006 I filed with the Iowa Ethics and Campaign Finance Disclosure Board personal financial disclosures, fundraising, and Team Development's, my consulting company, sale of goods to a political subdivision of the State for commission sales. From my understanding of the law and Senate regulations, as well as my longtime experience in the Legislature, I was totally transparent with the State as to my business activities.

Changes in my business

Things among my Personal Security Plus business associates and I began to change around April 5, 2006. On that date Marc Beltrame e-mailed Eric Brewer, "We (Matt & I) met for coffee yesterday and Matt shared some serious concerns about our venture for the first time."

Returned E-mail from Eric to Marc, "...Matt and you need to be 100% sure going into this deal."

Marc back again to Eric on the same day, "I couldn't agree with you more. As you know, I have had some reservations all along. It has been my sense that you have as well. Things sort of changed along the way once Tom revealed himself. If we could find a solid character with good experience to run the business I am 100% on board. In the absence of that I think it is an unnecessary risk to Matt and myself..."

Accessing our communications

Someone accessing these e-mails, or listening to our telephone conversations, could logically infer the planned business involving the FBI's stooge and I was going down. The FBI had to act fast to bring this to a head before we booted Tom, thereby destroying their case that Tom was being extorted. You don't eliminate your cash cow--the person you are extorting money from--if in fact you are guilty of extortion.

I was clueless as to what was really going on.

Two days after these e-mails were exchanged the FBI visited both Beltrame and me. In view of the timing, I now believe our communications were accessed by the FBI.

Gray's Lake Ride

At a Sunday night AA meeting I ran into Tom. He inquired, "Why haven't you called me?" I answered, "Well geez Tom you know with all that is going on related to this investigation I just didn't think it was appropriate. Do you know any more?" He led me to believe that somehow, he had the power to make this thing go away by going to the person who got the whole process started. I think that person was his friend Lieutenant Terry Mitchell. My lawyers had advised me to encourage Tom to come in to talk with them because they wanted to get information on what he knew about what was going on. Tom could help them piece this mess together.

On June 13, 2006 Tom met with me. I decided I would go ahead and risk one more interaction with Tom to see if he could shed some light on what was taking place. Tom asked if I wanted to get together for coffee. I said I really didn't want to go anywhere I could be tape recorded. At the time I still believed when I was being tape recorded in restaurants it done with a hidden microphone or some type of listening device. There were devices capable of recording with precision a conversation from 200 feet away. Instead of going for coffee, Tom offered to pick me up to go for a ride. So, we did. He drove to Gray's Lake, a popular park and lake near downtown Des Moines. As he drove around the lake, we visited.

About mid-way through our conversation I definitely knew he was the heartless rat. I knew this man, who lacked a soul, had done me dirty. I sensed he was suffering from clear recollection of key facts along with the truth. He was playing me very hard. I remember wanting to get out of the car but not before I had a chance to make my case. I knew Tom was probably the culprit. I also knew he was going to personally report our conversation to the FBI. If I was being secretly taped recording me again this might be my one chance to tell my side of the story. Again, I tried to methodically go through the facts as I knew them to be. The truth. Tom wasn't biting. Unbeknownst to me he was on the FBI's payroll.

He was working for the home team whose goal was to entrap me. He knew who was buttering his bread that day and it was the federal government that was paying him secretly, illegally.

I knew I had to control myself, control my emotions and as much as possible remind him of relevant facts and the truth. Frankly, I hoped if that truth surfaced it would unwind this whole deal bringing it to a head.

Tom was very arrogant. I tried to make the point that this wasn't about the money, I had told him that. I had told him to keep the money as he needed it more than me. I even asked him if he remembered all that. Whenever I would get close to touching a nerve, he would hollow, change the subject, or talk about some girl walking by at the lake. He did all he could to try to throw me off course.

That was the last time Tom and I talked.

Vasquez's sudden wealth

Tom did okay throughout this. Although I'm not certain how much he was paid by the FBI, I do know that he used some of that money to purchase illegal drugs. He testified to this on the stand. Nice use of taxpayer's money.

On February 1, 2007 Tom purchased the house at 2009 Nash Drive, Des Moines, for $110,000 (County Assessor's Records). Down payment on his modest residence was $25,000. The house later went into a bankruptcy sale. Tom also cleared-up $8,500 in back child support. I have not been able to determine the source of his sudden wealth.

Official Photo of U.S. Acting Attorney General
Matthew G. Whitaker.
At the time of my trial he was U.S. Attorney
Southern District of Iowa.
(Photo in the Public Domain)

Longtime friend and my Defense Attorney Jerry Crawford and me.

Marc Beltrame, my attorney and friend, who was to partner in our new company for home monitoring systems. He was visited by the FBI in the early morning hours at exactly the same time two other agents were at my door.

Co-author Jim Ferguson and his wife Jill, a retired high school and college instructor. They live in Clive, a Des Moines suburb.

At the time of my trial, I served as an Iowa State Senator. Here I am greeting constituents advocating specific legislation.

Soon after I was out publicly, I escorted Gov. Vilsack to the podium of the House of Representatives for his State of the State Address. I wore a pink tie and had a pink handkerchief folded in a triangle symbolizing gay pride. Pictured are the late Sen. Pat Ward, Gov. Vilsack, Jess Vilsack, and me.

My mom and I at a charity dinner.

Graduation day from Roosevelt High School, Des Moines,
for my son Jack. The guy with him is his proud father.

"If you are going through hell, keep going."
Winston Churchill, 1943

5

Indictment

24 FBI interviews seeking reasons to charge me

Documentation referred to as "503" consists of depositions taken by the FBI. A 503 was written for each person they interviewed. There were at least 24 people interviewed, there may have been more. The FBI conducts these interviews hoping to develop patterns, uncover additional leads, or create an evidence trail they can take to the grand jury. In other words, they do the investigations to provide evidence for the grand jury which then determines if there is enough evidence to make a charge.

Can you imagine having 24 people you know questioned about your integrity? Having them wonder why you are being investigated by the FBI? It not only violated my privacy it was extremely invasive.

The FBI's usual procedure was to contact the person to be questioned on a Friday to schedule an interview for the following week. I am sure this was to make me spend the weekend in anxiety and to make the person to be interviewed uneasy. Every week I would receive a phone call from another person who would excitedly say, "You're never going to believe what just happened to me. I just received a call from the Federal Bureau of Investigation." Oh yes, I believed it. This became an unusual form of torture by letting the stress they created with their calls just hang without a final conclusion. Many contacted by the FBI phoned me wanting suggestions on what to say. My consistent response was, "Tell them the truth. The truth shall make me free. Cooperate fully. We have nothing to hide." They were asked by the FBI if I had coached them. Had any of them said "yes" the FBI would have been delighted to charge me with witness tampering or obstruction of justice. Although most of the people interviewed gave me positive support, the U.S. Attorney picked interview summaries to be presented in court. I wanted all of the interviews to be presented and not left on the cutting room floor. This would emphasize obvious patterns of high character, integrity, and strong citizenship.

Those interviewed included:

Jenny McCoy - my former wife

Kerty Levy - my former boss, president & CEO Downtown Community Alliance

Marc Beltrame - my attorney and business partner

Dennis Shull - CPA

Jack Kibbie - State Senator, President of Iowa Senate

Dick Dearden - State Senator

Mike Marshal - Secretary of Senate

Charlie Smithson - Executive Director Iowa Ethics and Campaign Disclosure Board

Tim Brien - Polk County Recorder's Office

Eric Brewer - my accountant

Michael Gronstal - State Senator, Chair of Democratic Caucus

Steve Conway - Senior Administrative Assistant to President of Senate

Reid Schultz - owner of Quality Care, Vasquez's boss

Dan Geiger - ADT representative

Scott Johnson - my business partner

Joe Straight - ADT representative

Mike Barnes - my friend and former business associate

Mark Daley - my campaign manager

Senator Mike Connolly

Kevin Concannon - Director of Department of Human Services
Gene Gessow - Deputy Director of the Department of Human Services
Mary Bertogli - State of Iowa Department of Human Services
Gary Dickey – Chief Counsel for Governor Vilsack
Multiple staff members at the Iowa Department of Human Services
A contractor whom I had hired to tear down an old abandoned building

The FBI worked very hard trying to turn over the magic stone that would reveal something to incriminate me. They had the expertise and resources to uncover potential evidence. Didn't happen. And, because it didn't happen they had nothing to take to the grand jury. At that point they should have ended their assault on me. This should never have moved forward to the grand jury.

Personal witch hunt

My business partner and attorney, Marc Beltrame, had his own attorney present with him while being questioned by the FBI. He felt he needed to protect himself, not knowing the nature of their inquiry. He told the FBI they were conducting a witch hunt and the thing sure seemed to be personal.

Grand jury

The grand jury process is difficult for someone without legal training to figure out. It can be difficult for a trained attorney to make sense of its alleged fairness. I lacked, as I think most Americans probably lack, an understanding of how our court and legal systems actually work. What I learned about them changed my view of justice and the judicial branch of our government. My case was to go to a grand jury that would meet in secret. There would be more than 20 jurist, some who would be there to hear all of my case, some who would hear part of my case, some hear very little of my case. In the end, all would vote to either indict or not indict. What an indictment means is there are evidentiary grounds to bring forward a criminal charge. It does not mean the defendant is guilty. If indicted the case is turned over to a court for trial.

Under the grand jury system, the defendant is not given an opportunity to address the grand jury or to hear the evidence presented against them. As the defendant, I was frozen out of knowing any of the "facts" presented or processes undertaken. I did not know when they were meeting, or what they were discussing. I didn't know how or in what fashion evidence was presented. I also didn't know what evidence was excluded. Prosecutors present to the grand jury only enough evidence to indicate that someone mostly likely committed a crime. If the grand jury agrees, the defendant is indicted and turned over to the court. Clearly, my defense team had no control if lies were told by authorities to the grand jury. How they operate is lawful but awful.

Business relationship with Vasquez

How my business relationship unfolded with Tom Vasquez was presented to the grand jury. This included our oral agreement, work that I had done for Tom's company, and disclosures I had made to the State of Iowa. These disclosures included my businesses and the business I anticipated conducting with the State. My attorney Monty Brown emphasized the government's alleged version of the events was diametrically opposed to mine. Vasquez claimed that he had solicited my help solely as a State Senator; that I did everything in that capacity. That was a total lie.

Senate officials testified

Two Senate officials testified before the Grand Jury and later at my trial. They were Senator John P. "Jack" Kibbie, President of the Iowa Senate and Stephen Conway, Senior Administrative Assistant to President of Senate.

Jack Kibbie

Kibbie is a farmer from northwest Iowa who has lived in the same county his entire life. Senator Kibbie was a tank commander in the Korean War where he earned the Bronze Star Metal awarded for heroic or meritorious achievement. He is also a successful businessman who invested heavily in bio-fuels. Kibbie has been active in the Democratic Party for decades. Notable achievements by the Democratic Party under his leadership were passage of the liquor by the drink law and establishing community colleges. He later served 17 years on the Community College Board, 10 of those years as chair.

Stephen Conway

Stephen Conway was the go-to man in the Senate for any questions regarding ethics, protocol, Senate rules or traditions. He served as Senior Administrative Aide to the President of the Iowa Senate for eight years. Stephen has an undergraduate degree in political science and a graduate degree in health care administration. He spent years in health services including being elected to serve on Polk County's Board for Broadlawns Hospital, five years as its chair. Serving as senior researcher on the Senate Democratic Research Staff gave him keen insight on the operations of government. Although a Democrat, he was impartial when it came to interpretation of rules and ethics. Stephen was a man of integrity who could not be intimated.

Kibbie and Conway interviewed

FBI Agent Kevin Kohler interviewed Kibbie two or three times. Although Kibbie and Conway went to the Court House together they were interviewed separately before the grand jury. Conway felt less trepidation about testifying before the grand jury than testifying in open court. He explained, "This may show my own prejudice. It was clear that the grand jury was made up of individuals who had very little knowledge of the political process or public affairs. The questions that were asked of me showed that and I felt that I was able to convey what I wanted to convey more fully and with better clarity than in court. Their questions generally indicated a lack of understanding of the role of legislature, the role of influence and money in politics."

Kibbie agreed with Conway, "I commented this was my first time before a grand jury and nearly all of the jurors nodded their heads too. They were a young group. It was just like on some busy afternoon you went down on the street and you picked the first 12 people that came along. They were working class people who you'd go have a beer with, ordinary folks."

Conway felt very comfortable with the process, ". . . because the prosecutor, the women, told me exactly what she was going to ask me which I found very helpful. She didn't spring anything on me that put me on the spot. She said, 'This is what I'm going to ask you and all I ask you to do is tell the truth.' It was very impressive performance on her part."

Conway observed, "A prosecutor in the grand jury has a great deal of authority and discretion and can lead that thing anyway they want. I was very impressed with the way the government handled that part of it. I wasn't particularly impressed with the trial counsel."

Each of their testimonies before the grand jury lasted less than 15 minutes. Kibbie was surprised with the outcome of the grand jury.

Subpoenaed before grand jury

Among those subpoenaed before the grand jury were:

Marc Beltrame - my attorney and business partner

Jack Kibbie - State Senator, President of Iowa Senate

Eric Brewer - my accountant

Steve Conway - Senior Administrative Assistant to President of Senate

Reid Schultz - owner of Quality Care, Vasquez's boss

Kevin Concannon - Director of Department of Human Services

Gene Gessow - Deputy Director of the Department of Human Services

Tom Vasquez - my former business partner who became the DOJ's chief witness

Indictment not in my thinking

I actually didn't think I would ever be indicted. That's true. The mountain of evidence in my favor should have made an indictment completely absurd, a waste of time and tax payer's money. Reassurance there was nothing there came from my attorneys, my friends, and people close to the situation. Feds were going to have a difficult time indicting me.

Take a plea?

My lawyers offered me an out, "Look, do you want to plead? Do you want to quit? Do you want to say it's 'too tough for me' and just walk away from this? That's what a lot of people do as they feel overwhelmed by the power of the federal government. They just get frustrated and plead to get this behind them."

I was not certain if my lawyers wanted me to take that option or if they were testing my resolve to plunge into the massive preparation for a very public trial. My belief all along was the truth would come out proving my innocence. Quite frankly, there was only one acceptable outcome--acquittal. I was staying in until the end.

March 5, 2007--Letter to *Register* – McCoy investigation a misuse of power, money[40]

I could not believe what I was hearing when I viewed a television clip on an alleged federal investigation surrounding state Sen. Matt McCoy. The TV station had rushed to report rumors rather than authentic news.

Thank you for Jeff Eckhoff's balanced, straightforward article on the investigation concerning McCoy ("Consulting Work Was Part of Probe, D.M.'s McCoy Says." Feb 22) Eckhoff did his homework. His objective investigative reporting was apparent. Details were related without insinuations or judgments.

It appears that McCoy did everything right. I fear that what is happening to him could happen to any of us. This is a scary use of governmental powers as well as a waste of resources.

Jim Ferguson, Altoona

March 6, 2007--Birthday party's uninvited guest

Interestingly enough, while all this was festering we had a birthday party at Mazzoti's, March 6, 2007 for my former wife. The Italian restaurant was owned by the parents of my senate clerk. A man was observed walking back and forth in the restaurant. Mother pointed him out saying it was pretty strange to see him just walking around. She was certain he was observing us. Months later at my trial, mother pointed out that same man who had been observing us at the restaurant.

March 12, 2007--Confronting reality

Transitioning from denial to confronting reality came about through various conversations with my determined attorneys. I will never forget the call from the co-leader of my legal team, Jerry Crawford. He was working with the United States Attorney's office and reporting to me on the grand jury. Crawford stated, "This thing's not looking good. It looks like they want to indict you." I fought comprehending his words. My instant reaction was this was really going to happen. This is it. I'm going to get indicted. I was frightened realizing that my life and liberties were at stake. Within 24 hours my life was going to change dramatically, it would never be the same. I knew something very, very bad was about to happen to me and to my family. It was a lot like, I suppose, being told you have cancer.

March 12, 2007--"I expect to be indicted"

I learned that U.S. Attorney Matt Whittaker was planning to have a press conference on the day my indictment was to come down from the grand jury. Rather than remaining silent and let Whitaker's press conference shape the news, my legal team decide to go on the offensive by having a private conversation with *The Des Moines Register's* reporter Jeff Eckoff. The paper is Iowa's largest and is published throughout the state. On Monday, March 12, 2007 my defense attorney Monty Brown and I shared a one-on-one exclusive story with reporter Eckoff. Eckoff had demonstrated balanced reporting. In the past the guy's given me a fair deal. He's been willing to do the necessary legwork in order to get to as many facts as possible before writing a story. We told Eckoff that I expected to be indicated the following day or in the very near future for attempted extortion relating to the circumstances of the case that I had previously shared with him. Our meeting with the reporter was to pre-empt Whitaker's grand announcement of my indictment. I imagined how upset Whitaker must have been when he read that headline stealing his thunder.

March 13, 2007--Fed's last-minute panic seeking non-existent evidence

The day before my indictment the FBI had gone with panting breath back to Iowa Senate President's Assistant Steve Conway to find out if, in fact, I had really made full disclosures about my business relationships and my consulting agreement. Conway assured them that I had. If that was not what really happened, the feds wanted to bring a perjury charge against me. Here they were, running around the final hours before indicting me, scrambling like rats seeking to find something to match their desired charges. They were digging deeper to find a crime that did not exist.

March 13, 2007--*Register* announces that I expect to be indicted

The Des Moines Register's front page headline on March 13, 2007, the day *before* my indictment and before Whitaker's self-serving press conference, screamed, "McCoy – I expect to be indicted."[41] This was splashed across the *Register's* front page announcing I had learned that my indictment was coming down about mid-day on the day following this article.

March 14, 2007--Whitaker's press conference

Ever the publicity hound, United States Attorney Matt Whitaker staged a press conference March 14, 2007 the day I was indicted. He scheduled the conference for 3:00 p.m. in front of the Federal Court House in order to make sure he hit all the six o'clock news channels. At the press conference, he stood and proudly announced that I had been indicted. It was a very public event complete with waving flags. Whitaker wanted to show everybody at his press conference that he was the guy running this show. He was the guy that got the indictment. He was calling the shots. It was his show. He was going to indict me as we had announced on the previous day that we were sure he would. He did not disappoint us.

March 14, 2007--At the Senate during Whitaker's press conference

Whitaker's press conference was on a day I was on the Senate floor. This sensational headline resulted in my being inundated with phone calls and messages. There must have been at least twenty reporters pressing to speak to me. All messages were given to my Senate Clerk Sonny Giudicessi to schedule interviews with them in a conference room at the Senate. One-by-one, each reporter interviewed me asking any question they had for as long as they wished. It took several hours to do stand-up on-camera interviews with all four regional television stations. Also, present with their mics and recorders were the Associated Press, Radio Iowa, *The Des Moines Register*, *Cedar Rapids Gazette*, and the *Sioux City Journal*. A state-wide effort was underway with calls coming in from all over the state. News of my indictment was also being picked up by national organizations. Wild.

Indicted
March 15, 2007--*The Des Moines Register's* Headline

The March 15, 2007, banner of *The Des Moines Register* blared in letters ¾" high: **"McCoy is charged with extortion: D.M. legislator accused of using his position to demand money."** Heavy. I knew it was coming, but seeing it actually in print was terrifying. I read it a dozen times trying to absorb it. *Register* Staff Writer Jeff Eckhoff wrote:

"State Sen. Matt McCoy used his elected office to extort nearly $2,000 from a Des Moines security company according to a federal indictment issued Wednesday...

Wednesday's indictment capped a more than year-long investigation that, according to McCoy, included more than 10 hours of taped conversations with a business partner turned federal informant.

McCoy has denied wrong doing...The three-page indictment alleges that McCoy used his political position to demand money from two men involved in the sale of ADT Quiet Care, a computerized systems of motion sensors designed to let caretakers monitor frail senior citizens via the Internet.

Court documents say McCoy, after a meeting with state officials and representatives of Security Plus of Des Moines, demanded a $100 commission on each unit sold. According to the indictment, McCoy 'threatened to return to the state Medicaid office and ensure that Security Plus would not be a Medicaid vendor if payments were not made to him...'

U.S. Attorney Matthew Whitaker said it does not matter that McCoy, as one state legislator, would have had little or no influence in the Iowa Department of Human Services.

'Whether or not he was influential with DHS is not material to this case,' Whitaker said. 'It's merely the threat that was made to Mr. Vasquez and Mr. Schultz.'

Whitaker said he expects no further charges and 'there is no allegations that Mr. Schultz or Mr. Vasquez committed any crime...'

McCoy said he saw no indication of a problem until December 2005, when an ADT vice president allegedly told Schultz, about McCoy's dealership plans. Schultz subsequently balked at McCoy's commission, which McCoy contends had been worked out previously with Vasquez...

Whitaker answered questions Wednesday about McCoy's case on the day after U.S. attorney General Alberto Gonzales defended himself over the alleged political firings of eight federal prosecutors around the country. Whitaker, a Republican, denied any political reason for the prosecution of a popular south Des Moines Democrat.

'I do my job without regard to partisan politics or any special ax to grind.' Whitaker said, 'We kind of go where the facts lead.'" [42]

Well the fact is they did indict me on one-count for *attempted* extortion under the Hobbs Act, a federal antiracketeering law used in cases involving public corruption. The charge stemmed from my receiving payment of $1,800 for my promised commissions earned through legal sales to the Department of Human Services. Tom claimed I was threatening to walk away and take the Department with me if he did not pay me my commission which he claimed I had no right to receive. The FBI admitted to paying at least $2,200 to Vasquez for clandestinely taping my conversations with him. Conviction could potentially mean a $250,000 fine and 20 years imprisonment. I got indicted because the grand jury was fed a bunch of misinformation. The prosecutors did everything they could to make sure the truth did not see the light of day before the grand jury.

Documented evidence will substantiate and prove that I did not extort, give the impression of extorting, or threaten Tom Vasquez in a manner that would cause him to suffer physically or financially if he did not live-up to his business agreement with me. I did not make insinuations that my business with Tom was under the color of my elected office. Furthermore, I was entitled to all the compensation that I received from Tom per terms of our agreement.

I believe the system was stacked against me. It wasn't until I was able to go into court where for the first time the burden of proof was on the prosecutors. They had to reveal their sources and evidence in detail--unlike the Kangaroo Court they ran in the grand jury. Prosecutors before the grand jury have the responsibility to do the right thing. However, in my case they did the most corrupt and criminal things by making sure the grand jurors never got the full story, never got the facts, and never got the truth. The prosecutors knew they did not have a lot with which to work. That is why, after all their tireless work and endless expenditure of tax payer funds, all they could come up with was only one count of attempted extortion.

I was facing twenty years in prison. I had no idea what life in prison would be like. I knew I would hate every minute of confinement. I knew it would be tough. Most difficult would be separation from my son. That was what I was thinking about--how to handle that. I had to make decisions about whether I wanted him to visit me in prison. I actually talked to my attorney about it. He recommended that we not expose Jack to the prison environment because there was a lot of ugliness. I understood it would have been absolutely miserable.

Criminal charges were foreign to my life experiences

To be charged with a crime was a totally foreign experience. It was difficult to encounter. I have received a variety of honors in my life from the time I became an Eagle Scout at the age of 15. My biography screams integrity–serving five years on the Polk County Conservation Board, serving as vice president of the Downtown Community Alliance, working for a Fortune 500 Company, working in the Chamber of Commerce, serving on the Board of Managers of Central Iowa YMCA, being on the Board of Directors for the Iowa Council of International Understanding, and being active on the Board of Directors for Youth Emergency Services & Shelter. I am a graduate of the Des Moines Leadership Institute, one of the youngest people to be elected to the Iowa State Legislature at age 26, a two-term member of the Iowa House of Representatives, and at the time, I was in my third term in the Iowa Senate. I spent my life building my reputation and then to see it torn apart because of false accusations levied by a friend and business partner was a very hurtful and terrifying experience

March 15, 2007--Press goes after Whitaker

Columnists took objective views of what took place. Early-on, *The Des Moines Register's* David Yepsen grasped the nuances of the drama, "It appears the U.S. attorney, Matt Whitaker, is aggressively going after the city's south-side Democratic organization and the way it does business. He recently indicted former south-side Des Moines City Council member Archie Brooks in connection with the CIETC scandal. Anyone familiar with southside politicians understands that making threats--or at least huffing and puffing with a lot of salty bravado--is a way of life for them. That may be what got McCoy into trouble, Whitaker is not just any Republican, but a socially conservative one. We now have the specter of a politically ambitious, evangelical Republican, with ties to the religious right going after a gay Democrat. Does this seem fair? Even if Whitaker has the goods on a south-side political kingpin like McCoy, there will always be those who wonder whether his actions are driven more by his desire to ferret out public corruption, his own political ambition or a dislike for McCoy's sexual orientation. Given the controversy unfolding in Washington over the politicization of the U.S. Justice Department, perhaps Whitaker should step aside and call in career prosecutors from outside to lead the charge against McCoy. This should be about McCoy, not Whitaker."[43]

Whitaker did not deny his interest in running for governor of Iowa in 2010.

March 16, 2007--Duffy Cartoon

Duffy cartoon Following my indictment there was a wonderful cartoon by Des Moines' cartoonist Brian Duffy in *The Des Moines Register* (March 16, 2007). The cartoon had a picture of a badly balding Matt Whitaker sitting at his desk, next to a large tape recorder. The name plate on his desk read "U.S. Attorney Whittaker." Next to him was a picture of his close friend and intimate, Alberto Gonzales. One caption read, "Similar to ADT we have our own computerized system of monitoring sensors." A second stated, "Senator Matt McCoy: I'm going to make you an offer you can't refuse." Duffy sketched a black cloudlike formation behind Whitaker's head. It seemed to symbolize dark gloomy days ahead or, perhaps more likely, that Whittaker was emitting a dark aura of evil. When asked about the cartoon, Whitaker, not wanting to give it any credence, or more likely failing to grasp its impact, trivialized it by saying he was not that heavy. It totally captured what was taking place. I am pleased to own the original copy of this cartoon.[44]

Brian Duffy, a cartoonist for over 30 years, was a longtime editorial cartoonist for "The Des Moines Register." He has been awarded two Best of Gannett Awards and two World Hunger Media Awards. Duffy has two books featuring his cartoons.

March 20, 2007--Lawmakers warn FBI on spying powers

March 20, 2007--"Washington--Republicans and Democrats sternly warned the FBI on Tuesday that it could lose its broad power to collect telephone, e-mail and financial records to hunt terrorist if the agency doesn't quickly address widespread abuses of the authority detailed in a recent internal investigation. The threats came as the Justice Department's chief watchdog, Glenn A Fine, told the House Judiciary Committee that the FBI engaged in widespread and serious misuse of its authority in illegally collecting the information from Americans and foreigners through so-called national security letters. Democrats called Fine's findings an example of how the justice Department has used broad counterterrorism authorities Congress granted in the wake of September 11 attacks to trample on privacy rights."[45]

March 21, 2007--Polk County Central Committee's Resolution of Support

Well over a hundred party activists attended the quarterly meeting of the Polk County Democratic Central Committee. Politics were heating up with the approach of the 2008 Iowa Caucuses and presidential election. Meetings such as this are attended by elected officials seeking re-election who want to make certain they have high visibility. Presidential candidate Joe Biden's sister Valerie Biden-Owens presented on his behalf. Representatives from the campaigns of Barack Obama, John Edwards, and Hillary Clinton where there to promote their respective candidates.

A resolution voting confidence in me and support for me was presented. The presenter of the proposal stressed that it was important that we as Democrats rally around to support our own; that we not abandon good Democrats but give them our backing. The resolution did not make a judgment of whether or not I was guilty of what I had been charged.

The carefully crafted statement was modeled to reflect Glenn A. Fine's statement to the House Judiciary Committee. "Fine found more than 700 cases in which FBI agents obtained telephone records through 'exigent letters' which asserted that grand jury subpoenas had been requested for the data, when in fact such subpoenas never been sought. The FBI's failure to establish sufficient controls or oversight for collecting the information constituted 'serious and unacceptable' failures."[46]

Two people spoke against the resolution supporting me on the basis of wanting the judicial process to play out. Four people stood tall speaking very highly of me. One detailed that it was obvious this was a set-up deal. A second person related in length about the hard, productive work I had done over the years and what was taking place with this indictment. Another person said she lived in my district and has worked with me for ten years. She went on to say that I got things done promptly, had an outstanding voting record, and strongly supported the party.

Polk County Chair of the Democratic Party Tom Henderson, who led the meeting, said he had intentionally tried to support me in the press. Therefore, this resolution would be the same thing he was trying to do. Henderson stated, "Senator McCoy has served the state of Iowa in an impeccable manner. Matt has always been willing to assist those in need, whether it is assisting his constituents with their problems or providing for needed health care programs for our less fortunate." Henderson was very supportive.

Resolution Supporting Senator Matt McCoy

Whereas for 15 years Senator McCoy has effectively served his constituents and the people of Iowa, and

Whereas Senator McCoy has had an exemplary record of high ethical standards and unquestioned integrity, and

Whereas Democratic State Senator Matt McCoy is currently under indictment brought on by a highly partisan Justice Department under questionable circumstances and using questionable methods of collecting evidence,

We therefore resolve to give Senator McCoy our support and confidence in the months ahead.

March 21, 2007

The resolution passed overwhelmingly. Only two "nay" votes were cast. These people wanted to wait to see the process through. Think they missed the point of the resolution.

Immediately following the meeting, my mother received supportive calls from folks who had heard about the meeting. Close friends of mine contacted me. This made me really feel great. It is amazing how important support from colleagues is when you feel everything is going against you.

Confident me approached reporters at court house

I believed all along that people would make decisions about my guilt or innocence based, in part, on how I conducted myself. I have always been a proud, confident guy and I was going to approach that court house confident, by myself, and certainly void of theatrics. This meant walking to and from the court house free of attorneys and speaking to the reporters with a daily declaration that, "I'm looking forward to the truth coming out and have been waiting for this opportunity." This was about how I was communicating to my constituents, colleagues, co-workers, friends and family who would be watching the news. These were the people who cared about me and I cared deeply about them. I didn't want to let them down. They were going to daily view a confident, courageous me approaching my trial.

March 29, 2007--Arraignment
Constant media presence

My attorneys had briefed me that I would be booked and have to go through process of standing before the judge to enter my plea. A bank of microphones was set-up by the media in front of the Federal Court House in downtown Des Moines. Stepping up to the mics, I casually gave some pretty standard things to the reporters like, "We're looking forward to our day in court and to getting the process going." But, I also added, "Look folks, I'm going to go in there. I'm going to fill out some paper work, do what I need to do, and then I'll be back out. If you want to talk after that I'd be happy to talk with you."

Basically, I approached interviews like any other media opportunity that I have long been accustomed to giving. Like it or not it was a media opportunity. The media was all over my case and would continue to be so. This was big news. It proved to be daily news in newspapers all over the state and on TV. You can choose any one of those media opportunities to have a good or bad interview. You can choose to have a bad interview, fly off the handle, speak in an angry voice, run away from the cameras, and tell the reporters to stuff it. But, if you choose to have a good interview, you have the ability to convey a message. My message that day was to convey the truth: "I'm innocent and I'm going to prove it. I'm looking forward to my opportunity to telling my side of the story and letting the truth come out."

My arraignment was at the Federal Court House in Des Moines on March 29, 2007 my 41st birthday. Some celebration!

All prisoners and people being arraigned are subjected to being photographed and fingerprinted. All aspects of this procedure were extremely degrading to my pride. No preferential treatment was given to me as a long-serving elected state senator, nor did I expect it. I had to leave my attorney behind. I went solo feeling alone but strong. It was almost symbolic of the disappointing abandonment by colleagues and some "friends" that was to follow. I was escorted everywhere by police. Doors and gates kept clanging close behind me. I was led through a series of holding cells into a booking cell. Jail personnel were courteous sensing my apprehension in being in such circumstances. There were other prisoners in the holding cells – drug addicts, drug dealers, and I could only guess who else. A United States Marshal booked and photographed me. Getting finger printed was a process where a camera worked each of my fingers creating a set of prints while I sat at a sterile stainless-steel table.

I decided I was going to smile for my mug shot. In spite of my feelings of despair, I refused to look like a victim. I wore a freshly pressed suit and a carefully selected tie. Damned, I looked good. I was required to surrender my passport. Although I understood the process, it was a humiliating. It was apparent they didn't trust anyone not to leave the country. All this gave me a sense of what it would be like to actually go through the process of being held in prison. I was certain they would try to break me down slowly, one step at a time taking away my humanity, my dignity.

Prosecuting Assistant United States Attorney Mary Luxa

Mary Luxa reminds me of the shock re-enforcement experiments in college where she did her assigned job. If she did it well she was rewarded. If not, she soon got the message after the appropriate shock was applied at the right time. A conditioned puppet. Someone who follows orders for fear of being shocked. Someone who therefore lacks guiding principles, courage and moral compass to stand for what is right. She lied with impunity.

May 16, 2007--Prosecuting attorney not truthful with government payments to Vasquez

Now comes the good stuff. On May 16, 2007, my attorney Monty Brown sent AUSA Mary Luxa a "Brady" letter requesting: "The disclosure of any financial inducements, financial remuneration, financial assistance, or offers or promises of same to Thomas Vasquez in exchange or in consideration of his cooperation pre/post-indictment in the above-entitled matter."[4] The Brady letter requires the prosecution to turn over all exculpatory evidence which might exonerate the defendant a criminal case. This request was made because my defense counsel had been apprised of rumors that Vasquez was paid by the FBI to be an informant. These rumors arose because Vasquez had apparently bragged he was being paid by the FBI.

June 4, 2007--AUSA Mary Luxa lies in response to Brady Letter

AUSA Mary Luxa replied *in writing* to our Brady letter. Montgomery Brown received that letter dated June 4, 2007, in response to his letter of May 16, 2007. The letter received was under the signature of Matt Whitaker, by Mary C. Luxa. Luxa's letter provided a striking statement of what we were up against. That it was sent under Whitaker's signature indicates he presumably read and approved the letter.

Luxa stated, "There have been no financial remuneration, financial assistance, or offers or promise of same to Mr. Vasquez in exchange or in consideration of his cooperation pre/post-indictment in the above-entitled matter." That simply was not true. Vasquez was being paid. Her response to requesting information regarding Vasquez's use of drugs or alcohol during the period of 2005 – to the present was shocking: "We do not believe we are required to otherwise investigate or seek out detailed information regarding instances of drug or alcohol use." Had they done so it is doubtful they would have rested their entire case on Vasquez.

Luxa's response regarding Vasquez's criminal record, he "appears to have an OWI misdemeanor conviction." That was not the extensive criminal record we reviewed. She apparently sanitized his criminal record; probably to enable them to base their case on his accusations.

Luxa's response for information regarding "authorized 'wiretaps' by the government upon any phone number associated with Matthew McCoy." Although the request limited the type of wiretapping her response was broad sweeping, "There were no authorized or unauthorized wiretaps obtained or utilized in this investigation." Again, that was a complete fabrication.

Why would Whitaker allow this letter to go out under his signature? Why wouldn't he have required documentation for each of her response or at the very least questioned them?

June 7, 2007—Bill of Particulars

"The purpose of a bill of particulars is to inform the defendant of the nature of the charge against him with sufficient precision to enable him to prepare for trial, to avoid or minimize the danger of surprise at trial, and to enable him to plead his acquittal or conviction in bar (*to prevent*) of another prosecution for the same offense when the indictment is too vague and indefinite."[48]

Government's response to our motion for a bill of particulars

"Conclusion: The Defendant has access to a detailed indictment and has been provided with all discovery (including FBI-302 of witnesses). The only items not produced at this time are the Grand Jury transcripts, which will be disclosed one week prior to trial, by agreement of the parties. The indictment and discovery provide the answers to many of Defendant's questions. Defendant's requests are also in the nature of ferreting out the Government's evidence it intends to present at trial, and its legal theories. Such information is not the proper subject of a bill of particulars. The Government respectfully requests that this Court deny Defendant's motions."[49]

"State Sen. Matt McCoy will have to wait until trial to see how federal prosecutors plan to back up a charge of attempted extortion against him. U.S. Magistrate Judge Celeste Bremer on Wednesday denied McCoy's motion for a 'Bill of Particulars,' or more-detailed account of the allegations that McCoy, a Des Moines Democrat, extorted money from two former partners in a venture to sell an electronic system for monitoring elderly people.

McCoy's attorneys had argued in court that, after listening to 10 or 12 hours of conversations recorded for the FBI, they still were unable to 'see the magic words' that might back up any extortion allegation.

Bremer disagreed Wednesday noting that McCoy's indictment 'sufficiently informs defendant of the nature of the charges.'

McCoy's trial is scheduled for July 30."[50]

June 27, 2007--Paranoia sets in

Having been followed in my car as well as on foot, having had federal agents sit next to me at lunch so they could tape record my conversations created a sense of paranoia. Not unfounded paranoia, real paranoia based on direct experiences. I constantly had to be aware of those around me within hearing distance. I'm not sure this fear has ever left me. Once your privacy has been violated it changes your life. Paranoia creeps in.

I was having coffee with Jim Ferguson at Temple Starbucks in downtown Des Moines. Jim and I have worked together in various capacities since 2004. We sat alone at one of the small tables in the corridor adjacent to the coffee shop. A man entered taking a seat close to me at an adjacent table. Had I pushed my chair back three inches I would have hit him. Red flags went up instantly. We moved away from him. Didn't work, he stuck to us. Wherever we moved to get away from him he followed right behind us. He trailed us through the corridor, across the coffee shop to a public patio, and back again to our original table. We didn't know if he was seeking information or attempting to intimate. The intruder tracking us opened my eyes to the fact that they will win at any cost. It was another reminder the federal government's unlimited resources enabled them to pay someone to follow me, tape me, or observe me in order to crack my resolve.

A week later Ferguson and I were again at Starbucks, sitting in a corner near the entrance. The intervening time had passed with nothing new. As I was laboriously searching for words to express what was at risk in my life, I had taken a comatose position, completely bent over. Jim barked at me, "For god's sake Matt, sit up! You're in the middle of a primary election!" With that I angrily shot back, "I'm trying to be sure people can't hear what I'm saying." Jim apologized. I sat up. My stress was totally apparent to both of us as was the hell I was going through. The unknown was devouring me.

Privacy became a priority

I was definitely fearful. I hired a private investigator. I did so at the advice of counsel to learn more about my intended business partners Tom Vasquez and Reid Schultz. The investigator asked if there were things in my home that would cause me embarrassment if the federal government raided it. Privacy is something all of us prize and safeguard. Things I might write or say privately were not intended for the world to view. So, I prepared a "panic package" to throw in personal items like notes and things I didn't want to read about in the morning newspapers. Additional humiliation wasn't needed. Certainly, all of the things in my panic package were legal, but I wanted to keep my private life private.

Additional steps were taken to protect my privacy, the confidentiality of my conversations. While having coffee with Jim my defense lawyer Jerry Crawford phoned. His first question was, "Do you have a confidential phone available?" I borrowed Ferguson's cell to ensure we weren't being taped.

This fear was soon shared by those who associated with me. Routine phone conversations began with, "Can we talk?" Translation, "Do you think we're being taped?" Most exchanges on the phone or through e-mail were conducted in code. All notes and scraps of paper created during an informal meeting were collected to be shredded. Nothing was ever thrown into a public wastebasket. Jim and I were developing materials for the trial and for this book. Upon meeting me he would announce immediately that he had a tape recorder in his pocket. We meet weekly for about four hours in a closed conference room at Village Bean in Des Moines' East Village. The owner, Jennifer Heintz Trow, protected our privacy and kept our coffee cups refilled. She was a great morale builder. Coffee shops were my preferred places to meet people.

Conversations in public places were in hushed tones. Sometimes I would conduct conversations on sidewalks to avoid being taped. While walking, I would often abruptly cross streets or turn corners to check if I was being followed. What a way to live.

October 9, 2007--Attorney Brown gains access to file and FBI reports

At approximately 1:30 p.m. on Tuesday, October 9, 2007, Brown met with AUSA Lester A. Paff in the U.S. Attorney's Office. Paff gave Brown access to my file and provided him with Jencks materials, including copies of several FBI reports (302s) that AUSA Mary Luxa had not previously provided, as well as grand jury testimonies.

In addition, AUSA Paff provided a five-page Federal Bureau of Investigation document detailing payments of compensation to Vasquez by the FBI beginning approximately January 31, 2006. The documents reflect total payments through June 14, 2006 of $2,265.00. These documents state that AUSA authorized the payments.

Paff fulfilled his legal obligations whereas other prosecutors had put up continued barriers blocking us from information and materials we had a right to have.

October 10, 2007--Petition for Dismissal

On October 10, 2007, my attorneys asked the United States District Court for the Southern District of Iowa to dismiss Count 1 of my Indictment, attempted extortion.

The petition began with a review of the revolving prosecuting attorneys assigned to this case. Assistant United States Attorneys (AUSA) Mary Luxa and Andy Kahl were the original prosecutors in my case. Kahl withdrew, and soon thereafter Luxa also withdrew. (This was after June 6, 2007.) No explanations were given about their quiet departures. They were replaced by AUSA Lester Paff from Des Moines and AUSA Ann Brickley from the Department of Justice in Washington, D.C.

Brown filed a petition that stated my "Defense Counsel had received recent information that Vasquez was still getting paid by the FBI and expects to get paid more in the future. We believed the FBI was required to obtain local U.S. Attorney Office approval to pay their witness, and that the FBI was further required to notify division or divisions of FBI headquarters in Washington, D.C. of the payments to Vasquez. We further believed that the U.S. Department of Justice, particularly, the Public Integrity Division, would had to have been notified of the payments to Vasquez, and likely authorized or approved them."

My attorneys reasonably believed that when AUSA Luxa falsely represented to Defense Counsel that **"There have been no financial inducements, financial remuneration, financial assistance, or offers or promises of same to Mr. Vasquez in exchange or in consideration of his cooperation pre/post-indictment in the above-entitled matter."** She was lying on some order or orders from above, perhaps DOJ division(s) in Washington, D.C. itself.

Brown wrote further, "The intentional deception of Defense Counsel by the U.S. Department of Justice has injured the Defendant and his preparation for trial in this matter. Among other things, it has caused Defense Counsel to chase leads, abandon other leads, and generally discount information Defendant's counsel was receiving regarding the investigation and Thomas Vasquez. It has also caused Defendant to further doubt the government's claims with respect to other *Brady* exculpatory evidence requested by Defense Counsel. In Defense Counsel's May 16, 2007 Brady letter, the defense sought in item "K" the following: **The existence and contents of any non-judicially authorized 'wiretaps' by the government upon any phone number associated with Matthew McCoy."** AUSA Luxa's response to this request was, **"There were no authorized or unauthorized wiretaps obtained or utilized in this investigation."**

Contrary to the Luxa's written statement, Brown pointed out that "from approximately April 7, 2006 to the present, Defense Counsel have been receiving specific information from various sources that phone conversations and potentially e-mail conversations between McCoy, his attorneys Marc Beltrame, and

Jerry Crawford, and other individuals, had been overheard or intercepted electronically.

With the revelation that false information was provided to defense counsel regarding "THE" witness for the prosecution, the Defendant and his counsel reasonably believe that the information they have received, in conjunction with other proofs that can be mustered, is in fact true--the FBI has had some ability to eavesdrop or intercept electronic communications engaged in by McCoy with various persons, including his attorneys. Defendant believes that the interception of McCoy communications has occurred without judicial authorization and that such interception has violated his due process rights to a fair trial, has resulted in misconduct before the grand jury, and has violated his Fifth and Sixth Amendment right to counsel."

The petition correctly stated the government's case was heavily dependent upon the credibility of Tom Vasquez and his version of the events

My attorneys requested that an evidentiary hearing be held regarding these issues at which time the government disclose all documents of any description relating to their investigation or prosecution of me. This included including any compensation paid to Thomas Vasquez.

We requested the Court enter an order dismissing this prosecution with prejudice for gross prosecutorial misconduct. On November 27, 2007 the dismissal charge was not granted.

Gritzner & Whitaker Grassley nominees

U.S. District Judge of the United States District Court for the Southern District of Iowa, James Gritzner, was recommended to President Bush to be nominated judge by Iowa U.S. Senator Charles Grassley and confirmed by the U.S. Senate. Gritzner was a former Grassley aide. U.S. Attorney Matthew Whitaker was also recommended for appointment by Grassley to President Bush.

November 9, 2007--Motion to Compel Disclosure

My attorneys moved for an Order compelling the government to disclose, prior to trial enumerated items. Among the documents requested were Agent Kevin Kohler's rough notes taken during interviews of potential witnesses. Kohler produced no FBI 302 forms for several people whom he had interviewed. My attorneys believed that Agent Kohler's actual notes would reveal that witnesses told him additional information bearing upon my innocence, that Agent Kohler then selectively edited out of his final 302 report. The typed reports varied from Kohler's actual notes. Proof of such selective editing could be used to impeach the credibility of Agent Kohler.

In the summation, Monty stated, "Defendant has proffered evidence of gross misconduct by the government in the presentation of evidence to the Grand Jury in order to obtain an indictment in this case. The hiding of payments to Vasquez by the original prosecution team from the Defense, is corroboration that one or more government prosecutors and the FBI possessed motivations to indict Defendant for reasons other than based upon a fair presentation of 'the facts' to the Grand Jury. Documentation that one or more Assistant U.S. Attorneys told Agent Kohler or the FBI to leave out all the exculpatory portions of the December 21, 2005 meeting between Defendant, Vasquez and Schultz and then intentionally permitted Agent Kohler to falsely testify about what occurred in that meeting, is relevant and material to the Court's determination that the government has engaged in outrageous misconduct that violates Defendant's due process rights, necessitating dismissal of the indictment. The politicization of the Department of Justice is a matter of public knowledge and is well-chronicled. Documentation that the original prosecution team instructed the FBI to selectively edit out evidence of innocence will be admissible to impeach the credibility of Agent Kohler, assist in proving that he testified falsely at the Grand Jury about what happened on December 21, 2005, and will support Defendant's theory of defense that the government was willing to hitch their case to Vasquez's story, no matter what evidence existed to contradict his account."[51]

November 22, 2007--Thanksgiving

My family and I had agonized through the Thanksgiving holiday awaiting Gritzner's decision for his dismissal of the charges against me. It did not come down before Thanksgiving. We prayed simple logic or even fair play or maybe even truth would prevail. However, it didn't.

November 27, 2007--Dismissal of charge not granted

U.S. District Judge James Gritzner refused to dismiss the charge against me. My appeal based on prosecutorial misconduct resulting in inaccurate information going to the grand jury was dismissed. It apparently did not make any difference that witnesses were allowed to lie before the grand jury.

Judge Gritzer's statement

Judge Gritzner wrote in his statement denying the Defense Team's motion to dismiss the charge against me:

"While AUSA Luxa's lapse of memory regarding payment to Vasquez is regrettable and generated predictable adversarial suspicion, the Court cannot conclude the Government's conduct on the whole was outrageous or intolerable so as to demand dismissal of the charges against Defendant. Rather, AUSA Luxa's failure to disclose appears to be an oversight which the Government, via AUSA Paff, remedied by ensuring defense counsel obtained this material well in advance of the trial. Thus, even assuming the Court determined AUSA Luxa's individual conduct was improper, the Court could not conclude that conduct accused prejudice to Defendant such that it deprived Defendant of a fair trial because the material was ultimately disclosed on October 9, 2007, nearly two months in advance of trial currently scheduled to commence on December 3, 2007...the Court cannot conclude Agent Kohler's testimony before the Grand Jury was intentionally false in a material respect or that prosecutors should have recognized it as such...

Although Vasquez's testimony before the Grand Jury appears to have been factually inaccurate, the Court cannot conclude Vasquez intentionally falsified his testimony. Nothing in the record suggests Vasquez's account was anything more than a mis-recollection of the details regarding the 'cash is king' statement...Defendant's Motion to Dismiss (Clerk's NO. 60) must be and hereby is **denied**."[52]

November 27, 2007--Eckhoff writes in the *Register*

Jeff Eckhoff reported in *The Des Moines Register*, "U.S. District Judge James Gritzner today acknowledged a 'regrettable' lapse of memory by Assistant U.S. Attorney Mary Luxa but said McCoy was not harmed by the (her) failure to disclose information, since he learned what he needed to well before trial.

While Luxa's conduct 'generated predictable adversarial suspicion, the court cannot conclude the government's conduct on the whole was outrageous or intolerable so as to demand dismissal of the charges against defendant,' Grizner ruled. 'Rather, AUSA Luxa's failure to disclose appears to be an oversight...'"[53]

Why weren't Kahl and Luxa held accountable?

Beltrame theorized why Luxa and Kahl were never held accountable, "Andy Kahl was, as we understood, the lead prosecutor. He was a senior AUSA and running the show. Luxa was the day-to-day person. When I testified twice before the grand jury, Andy Kahl ran the testimony. When other people testified it was Mary Luxa. Luxa was the violating party and Kahl was her supervisor. Why weren't they both held accountable? I think because it would have been embarrassing for the government. As it turned out they both were very quietly removed from the case. That never was publicized. I assume Whitaker removed them or they removed themselves. I don't know. She went off. I believe she took a leave of absence after that."

My reaction to the tolerance for lying

In my opinion, the government can lie, cheat, steal, do anything they want to win the game. There was a Southside guy, who went to prison for lying about drinking beer and gambling at Prairie Meadows Casino. Yet Mary Luxa, who lied to my attorneys on a federal form, lied on a Brady violation request, lied in front of Judge Celeste Bremer, did not get into trouble. Judge James Gritzner said her lying was an unfortunate lapse of memory. But if I had an unfortunate lapse of memory I would have been cuffed and hauled off to prison. This was an astonishing miscarriage of justice.

Trial date set

My court date was set for December 3, 2007. At least it was well before Christmas.

My family and I had to realize I could spend 20 years in prison

I had to be realistic. I had to live my life prepared. What happens if it does not go the way I want? Fortunately, I knew my son Jack would be more than well cared for by his mother. Extended family was in town for additional support. If I was sent to prison I thought of having to empty my house, storing my things. Ultimately, I knew if I had to go away for a period of time (euphemism for "prison") I couldn't go away and keep my home and years of memories. What I was trying to do was not lose everything. How could I hang onto a few of my personal possessions and get through all this without being completely devastated? These were the things I was thinking about as I had to figure out how to stop the hemorrhaging of money.

Save the Pollyanna

I found that often times that family and friends tried to be supportive to the point of always taking the optimistic view. Pollyanna. I was like don't shove that on me. My life was at stake and it's phony. I didn't want to hear it. I didn't accept that gray skies were going to clear-up and all I needed to do was put on a happy face. Wasn't going to work. I was in a fight for my life and the only way I was going to come out of it on top was to deal with reality. I wanted friends and family to be prepared for what ultimately could happen. Ultimately, I could go to prison. There is no doubt in my mind I would have gone to prison if I had been convicted.

Senate Majority Leader Mike Gronstal's statement

Senate Majority Leader Mike Gronstal's statements, probably drafted by his staff, were shown to me prior to being released. I let him know they were wimpy. This is Gronstal's statement issued after my indictment:

"Iowans want, expect, and deserve to have their legislators function in a way that meets a high ethical standing. Senate Democrats are committed to ensuring that all our members meet those high ethical standards.

Naturally, we are concerned about the criminal indictment against Senator McCoy. If true, these are serious charges.

Obviously, like any other U.S. citizen, Senator McCoy is presumed innocent until proven guilty.

In consultation with Senator McCoy, we will continue to monitor this matter to assure there are no real or perceived conflicts of interest as it relates to his ongoing legislative duties."

Never enough money

The average person facing the enormous power of the federal government has few weapons going into battle against their unlimited resources. Although it is not impossible to confront them, it certainly seemed insurmountable. They put the average guy up against this gigantic team. It is a daunting process.

Expenses never stopped. Constantly, I wondered if there would be enough money to fight a decent defense. Fear of running out of money was unending. When going into battle, money is needed; it simply was the means to keep me out of prison. Going up against unlimited FBI resources required conserving money to ensure when push came to shove I would have the funds to go the distance. Not being a wealthy person, but having had some success enabled me to have the resources to do things other less fortunate people could not do. But I still needed a lot more cash.

Alone

In spite of having family and friends that loved me, I felt alone. Ultimately, at the day's end I was left in the darkness by myself. Despite everybody's best intentions and hopes, I was very much aware that I was going to be the only one sitting in the defense chair.

My colleagues in the Senate walked around me. In politics you realize that you have very few friends when you are down. That culture was alive and well. The fact is, when I was pressed against the wall I realized that I had very few friends willing to risk their careers to publicly support me.

There was an effort immediately to reach out on my behalf to elected officials both at the state and federal levels, people with whom I had a relationship. Many elected officials turned a deaf ear, handed their phone to staffers to return my calls. Even members of my own caucus were hesitant to extend support. At the same time when Congressional and Senate offices were asked to investigate this matter they too turned a deaf ear. Congress did not want to own up to some of the problems that were occurring, some of the excesses taking place, and some of the clearly outrageous dismantling of personal liberties that were occurring. No one wanted to be singled out as someone who would rather take a stand for personal liberty and freedoms over security. They stayed in the own comfort zones.

To say that I became defective as a person is not an overstatement. That I went from being an upstanding, "go-to guy" to being kind of a contagious leper from who people kept their distance. There were many people that said, "We know you didn't do it." Or, "We know you're innocent." However, at the same time few were ready to put themselves in a situation where they risked being publicly associated with someone who might be convicted of legislative corruption. Senator Jack Hatch, who sat next to me in the Senate, was one that stepped-up and stood by me. President of the Senate Jack Kibbie stood by me along with some others. A Representative for whom I had moved out of a newly designated District so he would not have to compete with me in the Primary, seemed to have forgotten that. My caucus didn't do anything. There wasn't a single day in court where one of them attended my trial with the exception of Jack Kibbie who was called as a witness. It hurt. Polk County Democrats and leadership were also scarce.

March 16, 2007--Strip me of my committees

I thought Republican Senator Mary Lundby way overstepped her authority when she wanted a vote to strip me, a Democrat, from all my committee assignments which would be tantamount to stripping me of any power or authority I had. "'This whole indictment is about influence and using influence. That's not to say he is guilty or not guilty,' said Senator Minority Leader Mary Lundby of Marion. 'At this point he needs to be careful so there are no more questions,' Lundby told reporters." [54] I was hurt by her actions. I recalled that when she had down times in her life that I tried to be a supportive friend. But when I was having a down time she didn't seem to mind piling on. I got her message.

Lobbyist quick to call my demise

There were lobbyists who wrote my political obituary leaving me for dead. The fact was that I planned to return to politics, run for office again and live to fight another day. This told me a lot about who was with me and who wasn't.

All in

Like the card player who pushes all the chips to the center of the table, I proclaimed, "I'm all in." That's what I did with my life, my resources, my reputation, my family, my future--all were tossed on the table. Anybody who has gone to battle with the federal government knows the feeling that it takes everything you have and then some. But this was one mountain I was ready to climb to save my reputation and to stay out of jail. I pushed everything to the center of the table with a simple, "I'm all in." I had nothing more to give.

"I am completely innocent of the charge against me. The documentation the U.S. Attorney possesses supports my innocence. This matter simply involves a contractual disagreement between two independent parties--my business partner and me. It is not a matter that should have involved the government in any way."
Matt McCoy, June 8, 2007

6

Trial

Preparing for trial--focus groups conducted

A focus group is a group of people that come together and hear the facts about a case. They hear lawyers from both sides of the case present the facts as they want them to be interpreted. An attorney from each side presented an outline of what they viewed as the major argument for and against my prosecution. It is almost like a mini-trial. My attorneys created two focus groups. Monty Brown was the defense attorney. Jim Quilty jumped in at the last minute to pitch hit, without preparation, and masterfully performed the role of prosecuting attorney. At the end of the group each participant provided feedback to a facilitator to help my attorneys prepare for trial.

I wanted to have two focus groups. It was expensive as everyone involved had to be paid. Participating "jurors" enjoyed hearing their opinions valued. In spite of the cost, we had to know how jurors might react as they heard the case. What would they likely object to about me? What arguments were compelling to them? What arguments did they consider frivolous?

We conducted two focus groups on two different nights. One group was to test our case to be able to reposition our arguments. The second focus group was conducted to see if we had improved.

We learned folks are skeptical of elected officials. Consequently, we had to get through that hurdle. Secondly, we needed to be concise and consistent with our message. We could not have 15 different messages.

Examples of individual feedback from the focus groups.

Pro-Defense rationale:

Two jurors believed that offensive language (in the tapes) and locker-room banter is normal between friends, and in this case was not used to instill fear.

Pro-Prosecution rationale:

Two jurors said that McCoy's offensive language (in the tapes), use of the phrase "take him out" and the reference to an AK-47 were intended to create fear of harm.

Key points in analysis of groups:

All jurors in the second group said the prosecution's references to McCoy's past alcoholism and homosexual lifestyle was irrelevant and inflammatory.

Two jurors said the fact that McCoy filed necessary paperwork with the senate ethics committee restored some faith and confidence that politicians abide by rules and regulations.

Participants' anger toward McCoy decreased as the focus groups progressed. During the course of the focus group participants reported an increase in sympathy for McCoy.

Even though we had opportunities to bring a lot more detail into the case we stuck with major themes based upon facts:

(1) I'm the guy who wanted to own a business;

(2) I had an opportunity to do a business with a friend I knew through AA;

(3) There was an agreement between my friend and I on the business and my commission;

(4) My friend reneged on the agreement;

(5) My friend didn't want to be responsible for having contracted me to do work for him, which he gladly accepted, but didn't want to pay me what he had promised; and

(6) My friend threw me under a bus to the FBI for fabricated charges.

Videos of both focus groups were studied in detail along with the 19 pages of analysis submitted by participants.

Preparing for trial--Coordination of the legal team

The best way to go into a trial is with facts and preparation. My legal team prepared assiduously. Monty Brown led a well-orchestrated defense team with Jerry Crawford and Jim Quilty. In the office with Jerry was his Co-defense Counsel Austin Kennedy and assistant Brenda Klocke who spent an enormous amount of time focusing on preparing for my trial. Whenever we met in the office, Klocke was usually there before us and left after us. I know she was working very long days. Additional legal support was provided by their assistants and support staffs. They literally worked around the clock for weeks to keep my freedom.

Home base for the legal team was Crawford's law firm because of its wonderful offices and great conference rooms. One room was literally dedicated as the McCoy War Room containing all the work documents, files, and evidence of my trial.

Our goal during preparation was to determine who was going to do what and who was going to say what. There was an enormous amount of time put into reviewing details, facts, information and double checking everything. Nothing was left to chance. Everything was vetted. Tension varied. At times it was very high and at other times things were jovial. It varied depending on the pressure we sensed. For fully two weeks leading up to the trial I had 100% of their attention.

The preparatory time was intense. We could not leave a stone unturned. We had a timeline and lists of things that we were trying to accomplish each day and by the end of the day those were done. We dissected Vasquez's 12 hours of tape transcripts. We spent so much time reviewing them that I swear I knew by heart every single transcript.

"Who said what?" "When you said this, what did you mean?" Crawford and Brown would both quiz me. "Well what were you trying to say when you said this?" "What did you mean by this?" I had to put it in context with the whole conversation.

Crawford would go home at night with talking points and arguments that he actually committed to memory. Which was a fascinating style of trying a case. He knew exactly what he was going to ask without referring to notes.

Jim Quilty

At the time of my trail, Jim Quilty was Crawford's law partner. He graduated magna cum laude from the University of Illinois Law School. During the trial, Quilty deposed people and questioned witnesses. He maintained the records for the trial which was extremely important and complicated. There were five Banker boxes full of files and records. These were highly organized with color codes and coordinated according to topic. Paper had to move instantly when needed. Jim could pull up a document for use during trial within seconds. Jim is a highly intelligent hard worker who was willing to put in whatever it took for us to win. This meant a lot of sleepless nights away from family. Going into federal court was like David taking on Goliath.

Grand jury transcripts of tapes

After reviewing what the grand jury had heard on the recorded tapes, we realized the federal prosecutors had taken all of the taped conversations, parsed them, and presented them out of context. So much of what the grand jury heard was parsed comments and statements that really had no applicability to what they were trying to prove. Parse and taken out of context the statements could sound bad but when you listened to the entire tape they didn't.

Proactive approach

My lawyers were extremely proactive. They were amazingly correct in what they anticipated was going to happen in the course of the trial. I think they were disappointed there was such a lack of preparation by Assistant Prosecuting U.S. Attorney Lester Paff and Prosecuting U.S. Attorney Ann Brickley. My team didn't feel the prosecutors were ready for the lines of questioning that they were going to have to do. I think my lawyers felt they needed to take longer with witness in order to make sure the whole story got told because so many times the government had no follow-up questions for the witnesses. Whether that was part of their strategy or lack of preparation, I'm not sure. I wondered if they were just lazy. They were probably not use to going into a bloody knuckle battle with top lawyers. These were government lawyers who were used to winning their cases because first, they were the government; secondly, they had the FBI; and thirdly, they usually had the positive ear of the courts. They got challenged by my legal team.

December 3, 2007--jury selection & opening statements
Federal Court

My trial was held in the large U.S. Federal Court House located at 123 East Walnut Street, Des Moines, IA. Even the name of the court house–FEDERAL–sounded foreboding. Although imposing, the building was probably constructed from standard government issued architectural drawings.

Courtroom décor conveyed a sense of the power of justice. The walnut judge's bench and jury box created a stately endorsement of strength. Corinthian columns supported the proclamation, "Justitia Omnibus," Latin meaning "Justice for All." It was over the entrance to an alcove with the seal of the "U.S. District Court-- Southern District of Iowa." The seal and statement hung against a marble and stone wall within the alcove. Pink and blue crown molding created an impressive finished look.

A sheaved sword supported the balance scales of justice. The balance symbolized the moral force of the judicial system. The sword symbolized that justice can be swift and final. We will see. It hasn't happened so far.

Three large flat screen monitors dominated prominent locations within the room. Electronics were ready to be used–Elmo, PowerPoint. In the front of the room was a glass enclosure safe- guarding a security camera.

There were three lawyers and three computers at the defense's table. Prosecutors had only one computer, two lawyers and an FBI agent at their table. Signs on their desks reminded them to "Please stand when addressing the judge or the jury."

The courtroom was funeral silent prior to the opening of court. Tense.

Hobbs Act

The Hobbs Act, which was the basis of my being charged, was enacted in 1946 to combat racketeering in labor. It is now used to prosecute public corruption. Areas covered are color of office, commerce, and extortion. Color of office occurs when an elected official obtains a payment to which s/he is not entitled but received in exchange for an official act. Under the Hobbs Act, I discovered the self-proclaimed victim, Vasquez, didn't actually have to have been extorted; he just had to say he *felt* economic threat and believed I had power to exploit him. In this case he felt I was going to cancel his contract with the State to sell Quiet Care and thus cause him economic loss. And, because I was a state senator, I had the official power to do so therefore coming under color of office. The Hobbs' scope is so broad they can convict almost anyone for anything.

DOJ's lawyer flown in from D.C.

We anticipated the arrival of a hotshot attorney from the Public Integrity Section of the Justice Department and the United States Attorney's Office. "The Public Integrity Section (PIN) oversees the federal effort to combat corruption through the prosecution of elected and appointed public officials at all levels of government. Section attorneys prosecute selected cases against federal, state, and local officials, and are available as a source of advice and expertise to other prosecutors and investigators."[55]

Prosecuting U.S. Attorney Ann Brickley, the attorney flown in from Washington, D.C., was an interesting study. She spent six weeks in Des Moines preparing for the trial. Alberto Gonzales' Department of Justice paid a pile of tax payer's money to repeatedly fly her many times from D.C. to the middle of Iowa's cornfields. Why? I haven't a clue. Was this Gonzales' attempt to intimidate local attorneys? If so, he didn't know whom he was up against. Perhaps Brickley was a favor of reassurance to Matt Whittaker.

Brickley wore the standard lawyer's pinstriped uniform that every male lawyer seems to own. She is a petite woman with long carefully styled hair. Brickey was so soft spoken that she was often difficult to hear. Several times the Judge requested that she speak louder to ensure she was heard by the jury which sat a short distance from her.

Brickley was to fall short of our hotshot expectations, in part because she was up against a powerhouse legal team. I'm certain she had not anticipated such a force. Brickley was under-prepared and clearly out-lawyered. Crawford and Brown had to be her on-going nightmare for months after the trial.

All this at taxpayers' expense for an alleged extortion case of less than $1,800.

Jury selection
On-line juror survey
Potential jurors were asked to complete an on-line questionnaire. The usual questions regarding name, address, etc. were asked. Additional questions that were more interesting included: Ever serve on a jury? Anyone employed by law enforcement agencies? Anyone involved in lawsuits or criminal cases? Any of you have relatives employed by U.S. government other than military? Any of you or your family members ever have claim dispute against government? Any of you already made up your mind about the case? Any of you have trouble with concept of innocent beyond reasonable doubt?

Our criteria for ideal jurors
We had our criteria for the people we wanted on the jury. We wanted to find as many highly educated or intelligent folks as we could. This was because my case was complex with a lot of issues relating to understanding conflicts of interests, Senate Ethics Rules and the difference between Senate Ethics Rules and laws. An understanding of Senate disclosure forms, tax liability and corporations required somebody who was fairly astute. I remember thinking the vast majority of folks in the jury pool were excellent candidates. There were a few that I knew I didn't want based on jobs they had had or their backgrounds. There were some people who worked for churches who were very religious, anti-gay and who articulated a philosophy that we didn't want.

When I read the bios of potential jurors I remember working to find out as much information as I could about each juror. I wanted to know about anything that was publicly available in the way of voter registration, where they lived, if they had done anything in the community, who they worked for and any relevant demographics.

After the total available jury pool had been reduced, it took less than an hour for the jury to be selected. We got an excellent jury.

Judge questioning jurors

Judge Gritzner reminded the jurors to, "Treat law enforcement testimony just like any other witness." He then asked:

"Anything occur to you that you might not be appropriate to sit on this case?"

"Any of you believe the Senator or this case has anything to do with CETET (a current scandal within the city involving major corruption in office of State Workforce Development)?"

"Anyone have moral beliefs that prevent you from passing judgment on another?"

"If you are informed that one or more people may be gay, will that make it difficult for you in considering this case?"

"You will hear recordings in which profanity is frequently used. Anyone believe they would be so upset by it that you could not be fair and impartial?"

"Will you be able to render a decision solely on the evidence?"

Prosecutor Paff's questions included:

"Any person having difficulty judging evidence covertly taped?"

"Anyone have a problem, or would not believe a witness because they have been paid? Any issue with this?"

Defense Attorney Monty Brown's Questions:

Brown opened his questioning with, "Hit beyond reasonable doubt--decide case solely on evidence." His line of questioning was framed to educate jurors on what they should do. Monty's homey, folksy approach belied his razor-sharp mind. He shared with the jurors that today was his father's birthday, building likeable connections with the jury.

"Anyone who does not feel they could judge another human being?"

"Do you understand real courts and TV courts are different?"

"Would you want to hear strong and vigorous questions about people who have some negative things about McCoy?"

Monty put jurors in Matt's shoes:

"Can you have your 'button' pushed?"

"Can two men who are friends take advantage of another's personality flaws?"

"Are you involved in small business? Have you done any business based on a handshake?"

"Do men in social settings speak differently to each other?"

"How many acres do you farm? 5,000 acres? I use to walk beans and de-tassel. They still do it."

"Ever involved in conversation where the person had a hidden agenda? Trying to get you to do something?"

Monty presented several scenarios, followed by asking jurors to end the sentence with yes/no responses.

Paff periodically objected–but each time he was overruled.

Key players in Court Room

Key participants in the trial included:

Federal Judge James Gritzner

Prosecuting Assistant U.S. Attorney Lester Paff, Des Moines

Prosecuting U.S. Attorney Ann Brickley, Department of Justice, Washington, D.C.

Prosecuting FBI Agent Kevin Kohler

Prosecutors' star witness Thomas Vasquez

Defense Attorney Jerry Crawford

Defense Attorney F. Montgomery (Monty) Brown

Defense Attorney Jim Quilty

Co-defense Counsel Austin Kennedy

Defendant Matt McCoy

Not physically present but very much in charge of the prosecutors and case was U.S. Attorney Matt Whitaker whose office was in same Court House as the trial.

Those sitting in the gallery throughout the trial were mainly members of my family, friends, lawyers, law students, and reporters. My former wife attended every day of my trial. She was positive, supportive, optimistic, and a great source of strength to me. Television cameras were not permitted in the courtroom.

December 3, 2007 (2:44 p.m.) Judge's instructions to the jury

Once the jury was seated, Judge Gritzner instructed them: "Indictment is simply an accusation--it is not proof. Your duty to find the evidence. You use reason and common sense. You must follow law--whether you agree with it or not. The attorney's opening statement is a summary of what they expect evidence to do. The Government must prove beyond reasonable doubt a crime was committed:

- McCoy attempted to induce Vasquez to part with money. He did so by fear of extortion (fear of economic harm). His action affected commerce: (a) Fear of economic loss or injury; (2) McCoy acted under color of official rite (taking money or property not due him through power of his office, that he could take or withhold some official action).
- Burdon of proof is beyond reasonable doubt on the prosecution.
- This does not mean prove beyond all doubt.
- Do not allow sympathy or prejudice to influence you."

I listened intently to every syllable uttered by the Judge. I faced 20 years in jail and a fine of $250,000 if convicted. The jailer was less captivated as he nodded off.

Prosecuting Assistant U.S. Attorney Lester Paff

Paff was short, intense, with a gravelly voice. His baggy trousers were piled on top of his un-shined shoes. His questioning was often at snail's pace. At times witness corrected his questions or impressions and even re-directed him.

Pam Whitmore, chair of the jury, later observed, "Paff was not as polished as the defense attorneys. Maybe their mission was a little different. Their pay may have been a little different. He wasn't as harsh. He wasn't afraid to ask questions but his tone of voice was a little bit more subdued. He didn't get agitated or worked-up. He was just kinda blah. He did not have the fire that the defense lawyers had. I think he thought he was well-prepared. But as the trial went on you began to see some flaws and cracks in some of the things they presented. They didn't have the material tied together."

Pam had been a teacher and later entered the healthcare field. She died on May 29, 2018 at the age of 77. Although I personally didn't know her, I attended her celebration of life at Christopher's Restaurant in quiet gratitude for what she meant in my life.

An attorney friend of Ferguson who had worked with Lester Paff for years described him as intelligent, aggressive (*that is a positive not a negative description*), skillful, hard worker, and very ethical. He was tough. Paff was given very difficult cases because he was a bulldog. He did not pass them off to others. There are lot of negative attitudes towards prosecutors because of the very nature of their role but Paff had integrity.

Paff 's opening statement

Paff opened with the time period for the alleged attempted extortion which was September 2, 2005 – April 7, 2006. According to the Hobbs Act's criteria for extortion I was not entitled to funds, Vasquez feared economic harm, and I was acting under official color of my office. Paff went on to provide alternate facts stating I demanded $100 for each unit sold or I'd go to the Department of Human Services and have them withhold support for Medicaid. If that were to happen, it would cancel what could have been a lucrative client for Vasquez.

Paff went on to say Vasquez felt something inappropriate and illegal was happening. He was put in contact with FBI Agent Kevin Kohler who arranged for Vasquez to tape record ten meetings with McCoy.

Paff also cited wild projections of what they said we could sell making me rich.

Paff assured the jury they would see the allegations are true and I was guilty of extorting money, color of office, and commerce.

A strange, but critical aspect of the Hobbs Act is that the "victim" does not actually have to have experienced extortion but just feared it.

Crawford's opening statement for the defense

Jerry Crawford led my legal team in giving the opening statement for my defense. His opening statements were completely devastating to the prosecution. He literally annihilated their case.

Crawford described Tom Vasquez as a charismatic con man. That Tom filed for bankruptcies, left financial victims in his wake, and used money provided by the FBI to purchase illegal drugs. Tom was:

dishonest,

a user of illegal drugs,

untrustworthy,

chronically behind in child support,

intensely motivated by greed, and

a very troubled man.

McCoy on the other hand ran in nine successful elections for the state legislature. In 2006, he received 70% of votes cast. He is a father who has always paid child support, has no criminal record, is an entrepreneur, and comes from a long-respected family.

Which man would you trust in making decisions in important matters of life? FBI Special Agent Kevin Kohler and the U.S. attorneys have chosen to believe Tom Vasquez.

Question--did Tom Vasquez agree to pay McCoy or did McCoy try to extort?

Agreement or extortion?

If you agree that McCoy was involved in business, then you cannot prove him guilty.

Relationship between Tom and McCoy developed in Alcoholic Anonymous. Tom Vasquez has been in/out of AA for 20 years, sober/not sober.

Honesty is one corner stone of AA. McCoy got honest about his drinking and stayed sober. Vasquez did not.

Their families know each other

Both are divorced, both have sons born one day apart.

Both worked out at the YMCA.

Both had a strong desire to help each other.

Vasquez attempted to use McCoy in same way he used others.

Vasquez used Matt when Matt thought he was his friend.

McCoy is a hard worker. That is different from Vasquez.

Tom Vasquez is not a worker. He is interested in schemes.

McCoy as a State legislator is paid $25,000 a year.

Paff: "Objection."

Judge: "You're suggesting a lot of evidence to be presented."

Crawford continued with the defense's opening statement.

Do witnesses say the same thing before grand jury and now?

Vasquez couldn't remember if he had testified once or twice before U.S. Grand Jury in a Federal Court House.

Oral agreements are enforceable contracts.

Tom Vasquez offered several other people to sell Quiet Care for $100 per unit.

FBI and the Federal government hadn't bothered to ask.

McCoy took Tom Vasquez up on his suggestion to start their own company.

So, Vasquez and McCoy enter into this oral agreement or contract and move forward.

This is crucial: Vasquez will come into this courtroom and deny there was ever any such agreement, deny that he offered McCoy $100 per unit.

Now, if Vasquez denied offering McCoy $100 and said McCoy extorted that money out of him you'd have to decide who was telling the truth.

But if you knew that this $100 per unit was exactly the same amount of Vasquez had offered numerous other persons to help sell this same product you'd have a completely different view of it right? In other words, this is just business as usual...why would anyone think this is odd or unusual or wrong to offer McCoy the same thing in his private capacity as a consultant?

Here is the problem and here is the outrage. Until 13 days ago, during a hearing in this building the federal government, the FBI, and the US Attorney hadn't even bothered to ask Vasquez, who worked with them to get an indictment against McCoy over his $100 per unit deal, if he had made exactly the same offer to other people. $100 per unit.

And Vasquez, under oath 13 days ago, admitted he had made this same offer to other people of $100 per unit that he made to McCoy.

Folks, that is just the way Vasquez is. He uses, or attempts to use, everyone who comes in his path.

In fact, keep this little question in the back of your mind as witnesses come before you: Does anyone come into this courtroom and say I did business with Vasquez and he was a stand-up guy, a hard worker, a guy whose word you could depend on?

The FBI, the Department of Justice, and the US Attorney have been working on this case two years this Thursday, two years to find one solitary witness who will come into this court room and say they did business with him and he was a hard worker and a straight shooter. Let's see if it happens.

And they have no excuses if they don't come up with someone. Because the evidence will show that Mr. Brown (co-defense attorney) and I went to the US Attorneys who used to be working on this case and the FBI agent BEFORE the grand jury returned an indictment and we told them about Vasquez.

We said look, we know you are sitting there thinking well this is just what McCoy's lawyers are saying about Vasquez so you folks do this. Go find any five people who know this guy, any five people he has done business with, any five people he has been in AA with and you ask those five people THAT YOU CHOOSE WHAT DO YOU THINK OF Vasquez? What do you think of his honesty, his work ethic, his business practices?

And, they didn't do it.

Instead, they gave the grand jury some half-truths, some direct falsehoods, very incomplete information and offered Vasquez up as an honest and trustworthy individual that they, the FBI and the Department of Justice believed in.

Now I want to talk for a minute about some very important evidence in this case:

You are going to hear Vasquez say that McCoy began extorting money out of him and demanding payment from him after the second meeting at the Department of Human Service...around Sept. 2. In fact, the indictment the Department of Justice and US Attorney drew up says that was when it started.

And Vasquez said that is when it started in his first of two appearances before the grand jury on January 9, 2007.

Now ask yourself this: What happens when one person starts extorting another person? What happens when one person starts threatening another person? What happens when one person starts demanding money they aren't entitled to from another person?

Because that is what the government claims happened here. That beginning Sept. 2 McCoy was extorting and threatening and demanding from Vasquez.

And this is well before Vasquez went to the FBI.

So, if McCoy was threatening or extorting wouldn't you expect Vasquez to try to avoid him? You surely wouldn't expect him to pursue him!

But look at this (records of cell calls).

Cell phone calls made by Vasquez to McCoy and calls made by McCoy to Vasquez.

In other words, the guy who says he was being extorted and threatened couldn't get enough of it...kept going back for more, I guess.

Your common sense will help you understand what was really going on here.

Vasquez talked to his AA sponsor (by the way he has had at least ten of those, maybe more, because he can't keep his word to or with anyone) and his AA sponsor of the day was Terry Mitchell who happened to be a detective with the Des Moines Police Department and told him McCoy was demanding payment from him. It wasn't true but Vasquez had to do something to get McCoy out of the way.

Mitchell, according to Vasquez either wanted to be in the FBI or had some relationship with the FBI and Mitchell went to the FBI and told them a state senator was demanding money from Vasquez and they immediately wanted Vasquez to wear a wire and secretly tape record conversations with McCoy.

Robert Frost in his poem noted that the harder path--the one less traveled--is the one, in the end, that makes all the difference. And, as in Mr. Frost's poem, here Matt McCoy took the harder path, the honorable, ethical and legal path. And the path chosen by Mr. McCoy does in fact make all the difference and will lead you to make the choice of finding Mr. McCoy not guilty of all charges.

Highlights of the Trial
The trial began on December 3 and ended on December 13, 2007, lasting nine long days
I'll walk through some of the highlights of my nine-day trial.

Brother Pat flies in from NYC

Of the fourth day of my trial, my brother Pat McCoy flew in from New York City to be with us adding moral support. His being with us meant a lot to my family and especially to me. I'll always be grateful. Family!

Mike McCoy to fly in witness

Mike McCoy was a very supportive brother. I leaned on him throughout the trial. He was a great source of strength. He was also generous in his financial support. Mike was going to go to Missouri and pick up Michael J. Hinton, an important witness, in a private plane that he had arranged for because roads had gotten icy. Hinton did not know whether he could drive here to tell his story. The weather ended up turning bad grounding the plane. My brother worked with him to make sure he had an opportunity to be a witness in court. The man turned down the opportunity to fly and drove to Des Moines.

Michael J. Hinton

Michael Hinton was from Columbia, Missouri. We spent some time tracking him down. He proved to be very co-operative, a nice man. Hinton was in business with Tom Vasquez from about March 2000 to December 2000. His working relationship with Tom was "based on a handshake." "We didn't have a contract—things just evolved as we talked. We worked together every day and just talked--I'll get this done, you get that. Like buddies. I worked for him and I was to be paid 'x' for each deal sold."

Tom didn't hold up to his end of the agreement. Hinton was doing more and more of the work as they went along. Hinton put in $34,000 into the business. It was lost almost immediately. Tom disappeared. He simply closed the doors leaving a string of bills behind him. That was it. Hinton phoned and phoned him but Tom had disappeared and couldn't be found. It was like he had vanished in the middle of the night.

Hinter related that Tom always had a story to tell. He was a con artist. He was a liar, a cheater, a womanizer. Always borrowing money. Tom had no drive, he didn't want to work. He was always excessive--more drinking, into the bar scene, going to strip clubs.

Furthermore, Tom didn't pay bills. He didn't pay suppliers and other companies. If he wanted something he went into Best Buy and charged $500 - $600 with no intention of ever paying them. Some of their equipment came from Ademe in Illinois. They got stuck for a lot of money. Their installer also got stuck for money owed him. Hinton got stuck for $3,400 on the lease in addition to having lost his investment funds.

I was amazed with Hinton. For all Tom put him through, for the loss of a large sum of money, Hinton was not bitter. He had not allowed all of that to take over his life.

Jack Kibbie--State Senator, President of the Senate

Kibbie testified that each Senator fills out Disclosure Statement which asks who you are, what you do, and your income sources over $1,000. It does not have to be in detail.

When asked if people called Matt "Senator" in his private life? Kibbie responded, "Once a senator always a senator."

Senators are expected to hold an outside job. They are not paid enough as a Senator to support a family. Kibbie testified that as a Senator, McCoy had a right to take clients to the Department of Human Services. Nothing prohibited it. McCoy can take his personal company to the State to earn money from it.

Steve Conway--Senator Administrative assistant to Jack Kibbie

Conway testified that, "McCoy came to him asking if a senator could sell a product to the State--late 2005 or early 2006. My belief there was no restriction from his engaging in business with the State of Iowa. I approached the Secretary of State and asked him. I disclosed this to the FBI the second time they interviewed me. McCoy asked if he can make money in his capacity selling to State? Yes, he can do that--make sure they are on your disclosure statement. He over-disclosed to the general public, Secretary of State, and Campaign Disclosure Board."

Crawford recommends to defense they pull the case

During the trial Jerry Crawford, the wise silver haired sage, went over to Paff and said, "Lester, pull this case now. I'm embarrassed for the United States of America. Have you had enough? Can't we end this?" Lester looked at Ann Brickley. Ann looked at Lester. Lester shrugged, "It's not our decision anymore. We're in it too far." Ann Brickley agreed they did not have control over it. That told Crawford somebody in Washington or in Matt Whittaker's office was making the calls. I think they knew they were getting slaughtered in court yet they couldn't do anything about it and didn't have the courage just to walk away.

Vasquez stressed by investigation

Prosecuting U.S. Attorney Ann Brickley questioned Vasquez, "Did you enjoy being part of this investigation?"

Vasquez: "Not at all--Matt was a friend, someone I respected for some of the things he has done. We tend to be friends. This has been difficult on my family. His family."

Brinkley: "How difficult on you?"

Vasquez: "Stress throughout the whole time. Not being able to talked about it--could not speak in detail to outside people who were extremely close to me. After it came out in the public in March, I started to have problems with my job."

Vasquez "obviously didn't want to do anything wrong"

Tom Vasquez appeared in court dressed in a dark suit, white shirt & gray checked tie—nice appearance. But with his square shoulders, he looked uncomfortable in a suit. I stared at him throughout the trial, amazed with the number of people he had conned–including me.

Vasquez told Des Moines Detective Terry Mitchell that I was asking him for money. Mitchell told him that was not right. "I obviously didn't want to give the Senator the money if it was illegal (*that's rich*) but didn't want him to turn off the system," claimed Vasquez.

Vasquez uncooperative on stand

Monty Brown held Vasquez to respond to the questions, often stating, "That's not what I asked." Brown also held Vasquez accountable for his testimony.

Vasquez attempted to re-structure questions to his own favor.

Vasquez had long silences with his head down in responding to questions.

Vasquez answers attempted to change context of questions.

In cross-examination by Crawford, Vasquez had amnesia. "I can't recall," "I don't remember," were his responses to more than 200 rapid fire questions. Crawford skillfully and quietly injected, "Who has custody of your son?" To which Vasquez mumbled, "I don't remember."

Crawford in mocked astonishment questioned loudly emphasizing each word: "YOU DON'T REMEMBER WHO HAS CUSTODY OF YOUR SON?!"

Pure theater.

Brown asked Vasquez if he kept his weed in a tin can on top of his refrigerator. Vasquez didn't remember. That had to unnerve Tom--wondering how much Brown knew about his life and who had told him.

Everyone was completely befuddled by the fact that prosecutors brought this witness into court that was so incapable of remembering anything, including who had custody of his son. He was just completely unprepared for whatever reason. I'm not certain if the government prepped their witness. If they had, they didn't put him through the intense prolonged preparation that I had experienced. Consequently, they were at a real disadvantage. For whatever reason, they allowed Vasquez to be on the stand babbling incoherently for almost a full day without making eye contact with anyone. The press referred to the Crawford's cross-examination of Vasquez as "blistering."

I testified in my own behalf

My taking the stand in my own defense was unusual. Anything I said that day that contradicted anything that I had been previously discussed could bring perjury charges against me. There is no more "in" then taking the stand in your own defense. You can't ever be prepared for what might happen in cross examination.

Pam Whitmore gave her impression of my testimony, "He was pretty straight forward. He looked at the jury, he looked at the lawyers, he looked you in the eye. He was fast to answer. He didn't have to think. You could tell he was talking from his experience rather than trying to piece stuff together so it sounded good basically. So again, I think his presence in court was very professional. I know that he probably put himself in an awkward position to testify. But I think to get the record straight it did help."

Miraculous happening

The next day, Monty stood and said to the jury, "Something really miraculous happened yesterday, something very out of the ordinary, something very courageous." He was talking about my testimony and what happened when I took the stand because in so many cases they never put the accused on the stand. Putting the accused on the stand really opens them up for whatever potshots prosecution wants to take at you. And they took their share at me.

Whitaker & FBI given second opportunity to drop the case

As this thing was really beginning to simmer, my attorneys and I were continually getting together for round table brain storming sessions ascertaining what needed to be done to set this thing back on course. Crawford's idea was to just go in for a visit with the U.S. Attorney and FBI, "Let's leave Matt at home. Monty, you and I will go talk to FBI Special Agent Kohler, and U.S. Attorneys Luxa and Whitaker. We'll truly find out their misunderstandings, and then we'll set the record straight."

So, off they went. I depended on them to make my case to the FBI and to the Department of Justice as to why this whole thing was the boondoggle Brown described. And it clearly was.

This was the second opportunity FBI had to take an informed look at their situation along with U.S. Attorney Matt Whitaker and drop their relentless pursuit to create a case against me. They could have simple dropped the allegations and let it go, saving taxpayers a pile of money. Certainly, I wouldn't have been the first person who ever had to clarify a business relationship with the government officials. It would have been an honorable ending without bloodshed.

Their refusal to listen to reason illustrated they were like hungry dogs in search of a crime. Even though no crime had occurred, they certainly were putting enormous resources into it as though it were major.

December 10, 2007--Dad testifies

My dad testified. He did me proud. Really a good guy. Here was a proud father speaking from the heart. My dad was a sympathetic witness. He related that I had told him about the new business and that I had been offered $100 per unit sold. Dad was conversational, strong on his family and on our values. He related numerous family stories not focusing on a specific topic--"My wife is a wonderful cook. We have many large family dinners. The kids just love coming home." It was a heartfelt testimony. Without intention, or blatantly trying to, he endeared himself to those in the audience and undoubtedly the jury.

Paff went after him. Paff was clearly attacking an older man. He came off like a bully as his attacks lacked merit. Error big time.

About Vasquez

"The discrediting campaign culminated earlier this week when two of Vasquez's former Alcoholics Anonymous sponsors referred to him in court as 'a pathological liar' and someone lacking 'the capacity to be honest.'"[54]

Vasquez told his former girlfriend that he did not have money for Christmas presents and back payments for child support. She loaned him $3,000 which was never repaid.

Vasquez confided in his girlfriend at the time, that he was scared of losing the ADT dealership. That he was going to go to Des Moines Police Detective Terry Mitchell about me. He was going to hurt me, it was going to be big, it would be in the news, he would be the one responsible for it, and that he was going to do it through a Des Moines detective.

Recognizing Vasquez was vulnerable, the federal prosecutor Brickley plainly told the jury in her closing arguments, "The government is not asking you to take Vasquez home with you for Christmas. We're just asking that you consider his testimony." Columnist Rekha Basu picked up on that line, "Vasquez was so thoroughly discredited during the nine-day trial that you might not want to share an elevator ride with him–much less take him home."[56]

December 14, 2007--Defense Brown's closing

Defense attorney Brown systematically butchered each of Brickley's arguments. He castigated federal authorities for failing to check out a questionable informant. That Vasquez left a trail of human wreckage wherever he went was graphically detailed. Brown was masterful.

December 14, 2007--Judge Gritzer cuts Brown's closing short

Looking at his watch, Judge Gritzer cut Brown's closing short in order to provide time to give his final charge to jurors before lunch. He sent my case to the jury at noon on December 14. I had put lots of money and time into visual displays to help bring closure to the jury. I know Monty had some very important things to say. This was not a small claims case. Gritzner needed to understand that I faced twenty years of prison time and a quarter million dollar fine if I was found guilty. We had the time. We had wasted two weeks; we could have wasted another two hours to enable Monty to make closing arguments that would tie the case together. My lawyers were concerned about it. They put in an enormous amount of time - 50, 60, 70 - hours in planning their closing. They worked all night trying to make sure that everything was said that needed to be said. They had a tremendous weight on their shoulders. These were three fantastic lawyers who took my freedom and my situation to heart personally and this weight was dropped on their shoulders. Monty went days without seeing his family while this trial was going on. Both of these guys knew they had my life in their hands. They did not take that lightly. There was no reason why we couldn't have had lunch and returned for Monty to finish his closing arguments. We had invested $800 in visuals that were tossed aside. One of these graphics was hand delivered to Crawford's office at 3:00 a.m. and received by his staff. It was clear that Gritzner was ready to get this trial wrapped up and to move on.

Judge instructs the jury

Judge Gritzner listed the following rules for the jury to follow:

1. Select a foreperson.

2. Discuss this case with other jurors and try to reach agreement without violence to individual judgment because a verdict must be unanimous. Don't be afraid to change your mind.

3. If the defendant is found guilty, the sentence to be imposed is my responsibility. You may not consider punishment in any way.

4. If you need to communicate with me you may send a note through a marshal or bailiff. You may not tell me how your vote stands numerically.

5. Your verdict must be based solely on evidence and on the law.

6. When you have reached a verdict, fill out the verdict form and advise the bailiff you are ready to return to the courtroom.

December 14, 2007--Judge sends jury to lunch

Judge Gritzner sent my case to the jury who seemed to immediately go to lunch. So did I. This was the first trial day that I had been able to leave the court house at noon. Previously, I had been sequestered for lunch in the court house. My two brothers joined me for lunch at nearby Lucca's. Every eye was on me as diners knew that I was in the middle of my trial. Although literally petrified, I made every effort to appear as confident as possible. I must have been effective because an attorney working in the court house at the time told Ferguson that he had talked with me during my trial. He said that he was surprised with how calm I was and that I didn't let on that I had a care in the world.

Following a heavy meal of pasta, we grabbed a cup of coffee at the Village Bean. Their conference room offered privacy with good service. Coffee was interrupted with a call from my attorney telling me to get back to the court house as soon as possible.

Dad collapses

Entering the court house, I looked up the long flight of stairs leading to the second floor. Dad was slumped over, white as a ghost, being held up by family members. I panicked literally thinking he was dying. "Oh God, please no." This was my fault. I did this to him. Dad looked a hundred years old. Mom asked Beltrame to go with Dad to the men's room. Beltrame talked Dad down from his panic attack. We found a bench for Dad to rest but he insisted on going back into the court room, risking a potential heart attack.

December 14, 2007--Jury returns verdict

When the jury returned to the courtroom, the foreperson carried a piece of paper. She seemed to have had positive non-verbals during the trial, or at least so thought my defense lawyers. Jurors had reached their decision within 25 minutes and then went out for their free lunch. The first vote taken by the jury to see where everyone stood was 11-1. The holdout juror did not believe anyone would make a business deal without a written contract. That juror ran a large farm operation where all work or purchases were probably based on written agreements. He changed his vote when all the other jurors assured him they had engaged in business transactions that were based on either a handshake or oral agreement.

The jurors returned to the court house following lunch. Foreperson Pam Whitmore announced they had reached a unanimous decision: ACQUITTED!

Upon hearing "ACQUITTED" I was overcome with emotion. It was unlike anything else in my life. Nothing had compared to the relief and level of emotion that I felt at that moment.

First, I hugged Jerry Crawford. Then I gave Monty Brown a bear hug. I couldn't let him go; it was like hugging my security blanket. Tears filled our eyes.

Dad had been on my mind. A quick glance at the gallery to the check on him showed that he appeared to be okay, his color had returned. I was relieved. Overcome with joy, Dad wept openly along with other sobbing members of my family. I felt an unbelievable sense of gratitude to the jury wishing with all of my being that I could have thanked each of them for seeing the truth. To this day I continue to have feelings of gratefulness towards those jurors.

Paff's comments after trial

After the trial I don't think anything was really said to my attorneys by Brickley. She was emotionally disappointed and wanted out of there. Paff came over and shook my hand saying I had done a "good job." That was lame. Did he think this was a sporting event? Every aspect of my life had been on the line. Years of being in the public eye have taught me to take the high road whenever possible. I returned his offer to shake hands with a simple "thanks." It would be the last time we spoke or that I saw him. With the end of my trial, Paff had only ten months to live. He succumbed to cancer on October 19, 2008 at age 63.

Press Conferences in front of the Federal Building

"Outside the courtroom, Brown and attorney Jerry Crawford later stopped just short of previous assertions that the case against McCoy, a Democrat, was politically motivated. U.S. Attorney Matthew Whitaker, a Republican appointed by President Bush, previously has denied any such allegation. Whitaker declined to comment Thursday other than to note his 'complete confidence in the jury system.'"[57]

I left the court house immediately following the verdict with very few comments to the press other than to say, "At the outset I had told you I had the truth on my side. I am grateful the jurors found the truth through all the lies. I'm now ready to enjoy Christmas."

Jack is jubilant

Jenny and I drove to Jack's school where we pulled him from class.

"We WON! Jack, it's over!"

Grinning ear-to-ear, Jack ran into my arms yelling, "I love you Dad."

"I love you too. It is all over. We will never have to deal with this again. You're going to be okay."

"Misuse of judicial power to further a political objective of an individual or political party, is a wicked cancer upon our democracy."

"Those who place their thumb on the scale of justice, risk endangering the very system they are sworn to protect and uphold."

Matt McCoy

7

Whitaker's Assault on Democracy

Foundation for accountability and civic trust

We won. Yes, but the toll was horrific.

At the trial's end, I was physically and mentally exhausted. Fatigue hit immediately. I wanted to do nothing more than crawl under the covers and sleep, sleep, sleep.

My family and friends had been traumatized from being put on the roller coaster from hell. My finances had taken a severe beating. I had both public and private careers to re-build. In addition, although my constituents had stood by me, I could take nothing for granted. I felt I needed to take steps to re-establish their trust.

Unfortunately, or fortunately, I now knew who my real friends were—the ones who stood by me. This included my colleagues in the Senate, some were no-shows when I needed them most. Scriptures from Romans kept running through my mind that went something like *bless those who persecute you, don't curse them, and don't be overcome with evil but overcome evil with good* (Romans 14).

I chose to take the high road by "killing" with kindness those who had abandoned me. Work was a remarkable therapy. Throwing myself full force into my work at the Senate proved to be healing.

Overcoming stress took time. Sleepless nights continued as did looking over my shoulder to see if I was being followed. "Wrong number" telephone calls gave cause for pause. I confided only in a small circle of close friends who had unquestionably stood by me. It took more than a year for normal life to resume. Even today I have disturbing flash-backs of what I had gone through.

Whitaker has put his own personal political ambition first even if it was above the law not only in my case but throughout his career.

In my case, he brought a single count indictment for attempting to extort a business partner and the entire case was built on the word of his star witness who was a drug user, abuser of women, deadbeat debtor who even his Alcoholic Anonymous sponsor called a "pathological liar."

Whitaker approved spending taxpayer money to pay an informant who used the money to buy drugs which he admitted under oath.

Whitaker's assault on democracy

In our democracy we are guaranteed certain rights, liberties, protections of our privacy and property. Whitaker was the U.S. Attorney in charge of my trial. I feel the manner in which he handled it was an assault on my democratic rights.

Assault on my rights

- The biggest assault on my rights was that I was a pawn in a national thrust by Gonzales and Whitaker to attack popular Democrats at the grass roots level. This was done to create chaos resulting in Democrats being turned out of office and Republicans elected to replace them.

- The interception of my communications occurred without judicial authorization which violated my due process rights to a fair trial.
- The misconduct before the grand jury violated my fifth and sixth amendment rights to counsel.
- The FBI manipulated data to the grand jury and at my trial.
- It felt like I was being harassed–every week someone new called to tell me they heard from the FBI that I was being investigated.
- FBI subjectively edited interviews with family, friends, and associates. Positive experiences and statements shared with investigators never made it into FBI reports.
- I was covertly tape recorded in restaurants and in confidential AA meetings. Wires were strapped to a confident whom I trusted--all done in the name of justice.
- Professional colleagues and acquaintances were pulled into clandestine meetings with the FBI simply because they made the mistake of knowing me.

Assault on my liberties

- The Hobbs Act virtually gives the government a blank check with sweeping latitude for interpretation and application. It can easily threaten individual liberties. It did mine.
- A US Attorney lied to the grand jury.
- The intentional deception of defense counsel injured preparation for my trial.
- My "friend" was paid by the DOJ to spy on its citizens.
- The government lied to manufacture a case against me.
- I no longer felt free. I was stalked in coffee shops, restaurants, parks.
- I lived in constant fear on being followed, being subjected to a home invasion, being sent to prison.
- I lost my trust in friends and colleagues. I trusted only family and a close circle of friends.
- I was continually intimated by the FBI interviewing my friends.
- My passport was confiscated.

- My son was bullied at school. He lived in constant fear I would be sent to prison. Nightmares were common.
- My parents were terrified. At a time of life when they should have been enjoying their carefree golden years, they were stressed with formidable fear of what might happen to me.

Assault on the protection of my privacy
- I was followed.
- I was stalked.
- It has been reported that my conversations and e-mails to/from my attorneys have been overhead or intercepted.
- I believe they monitored my phone. They said they did not but they lied about everything else–I assume they did about that. They knew too much.

Assault on the protection of my property
- My bank and financial records were analyzed.
- My tax returns were analyzed which I observed Agent Kohler doing during my trial.
- My e-mails were examined and dissected.

Overwhelming support from the community
Following my trial, the public was very positive. My phone lines were jammed. I couldn't make or take calls. My answering machine was completely full of messages. Everybody wished me well. Nobody wished me ill. Nobody said anything negative. The level of support I had from the community was overwhelming.

Project Safe Justice Video
Project Safe Justice is an organization formed to look at the Department of Justice and the politicization that occurred under Karl Rove and Alberto Gonzales. They were making a video of politicians who came under attack by the DOJ. Representatives of the organization came to my home to interview me about what I experienced as I went through my trial. What did I find the Federal Government's motives to be as we uncovered the fake charges against me and the harassment perpetuated by the DOJ and FBI? The purpose of that video was to expose the Republican Party, the Bush Administration and the DOJ, who will stop at nothing to

achieve their *Win at any Cost* mantra. Their video is a collection of stories from other public officials who experienced similar humiliation and harassment by the DOJ. These actions were primarily in the swing states in the last presidential battle field. The DOJ decided they would focus on weakening the Democratic Party so the Republicans would have a better shot of winning those states in the future.

November 8, 2018--CNN Interview

CNN knew through an interview with a local television station that I was falsely charged by Whitaker for alleged extortion. CNN asked if I would consent to an on-camera interview regarding Whitaker. I jumped at the chance to tell my story hoping it would prevent others from having to go through such hell. CNN flew Drew Griffin and his camera person to Des Moines to interview me at my office. The interview was aired on November 9, 2018. Its narrative may be found in Appendix B in the article, "Whitaker's controversial prosecution of a gay Democrat." My staff and I were impressed with CNN's professionalism, the precision of their operation and with Griffin's thoughtfulness. He said goodbye to each staff member thanking them for their assistance and for the courtesies extended to him.

A flood of calls immediately poured in from other media including *The New York Times, Washington Post, Huffington News, Boston Globe,* Google News, CNN, MSNBC, *Roll Call Magazine,* and *BLADE Magazine.*

November 8, 2018--KCCI followed CNN

Local KCCI television news commentator Lauren Donovan and her camera man Courtney Kintzer, director of photography, filmed an additional interview with me immediately following CNN's filming.

November 11, 2018--My article in *POLITICO*

POLITICO became aware of my vocal opposition of Matt Whitaker in his attack on democracy. During CNN's filming of me, POLITICO contacted me for an article detailing Whitaker's involvement in my trial. Perfect. What I thought would take a few minutes to hammer out their article evolved into two full days.

POLITICO vetted every word, every sentence. Everything had to be documented. I understand why they are so highly thought of and trusted.

It was therapeutic to be able to share my story at the national level in order to bring transparency to the sham trial they put me through as a way get rid of elected Democrats at the local level. It is a story I'd find hard to believe if I hadn't been one of their victims. The widely quoted article titled, "I was the Subject of a Political 'Witch Hunt,' Matt Whitaker Directed it." may be found in Appendix A. It was published on November 11, 2018.[58]

Columnist go after Federal Prosecutors targeting Democrats

November 2, 2007: Gilbert Cranberg, thought there seemed to be ample evidence of the federal prosecutors targeting Democratic politicians.[59]

November 9, 2007: "'It was a horrible case--it was made up-- and it was designed to take a high-profile Democrat, who was popular, openly gay and listed as one of the top 100 rising starts in the Democratic Party and smear me,' Mr. McCoy said in an interview. Kern Kupec, a Justice Department spokeswomen, rebutted Mr. McCoy, 'The allegations of improper prosecution are ridiculous,' she said. 'The Justice Department signed off on the case. The FBI investigated it. And career prosecutors handled the case every step of the way.' As a federal prosecutor, Mr. Whitaker continued to show political ambition."[60]

December 20, 2007: Marc Hansen wrote, "Most Democrats say politics was behind the prosecution of State Sen. Matt McCoy. Is there some smoking-gun in Washington saying Whitaker better go after more Democrats?"[61]

December 21, 2007: Rekha Basu stated, "It has all the earmarks of a politically motivated witch hunt...(Iowa) Senators Tom Harkin or Chuck Grassley can and should request access to correspondence (withheld by the government)."[62]

January 17-23, 2018: Gilbert Cranberg, quoted a veteran criminal defense lawyer who thought there was reason to suspect the case was another in a series of politically-inspired prosecutions initiated by Gonzales.[63]

Not an isolated case

My case was not an isolated incident. Over time, it became apparent that my indictment was most likely linked to the national scene. The eight U.S. prosecutors that Gonzales fired on December 7, 2006 were all held in good standing with the DOJ. Congress was beginning to question if politics played a role in it. Some of the fired U.S. prosecutors revealed they had been told by the DOJ to investigate certain individuals and to ignore others. Evidence in a July 2008, report investigating hiring practices for U.S. attorneys by the DOJ revealed their criteria included "God, guns, and gays." Interviews included questions on applicant's political affiliations, ideology and opposition to gun control.

Candidates were refused jobs because their sexual orientation was in question.

Invasion of my privacy

The invasion of my privacy was appalling: I was followed, my conversations were recorded, and my financial records were seized. In addition, family members, co-workers, legislative colleagues, and acquaintances were questioned. My e-mails were read. The e-mails and financial records of a business colleague were subpoenaed. I believe my phone was also monitored which they denied. I was in the middle of an election campaign and had they monitored my phones they would have violated federal election laws. But, they simply knew too much not to have been monitoring my phones. All this disrupted my life beyond belief. My family was in turmoil. My reputation and future were negatively impacted. Emotional stress took its toll on my physical and mental health. It negatively impacted my political career as well as that of all politicians. A vast amount of time was lost that could have spent more productively. I also lost actual and potential income along with my savings.

Federal pursuit motivated by my sexual orientation

There is ample evidence to suspect the federal pursuit of me was motivated by politics and my sexual orientation. This was undoubtedly part of a wider sweep by the DOJ. In one short eight-year period, it seems as if more than 200 years of Constitutional protections, personal liberties and freedoms had been eroded under George W. Bush. A complacent Congress lacked the political courage to stand-up and tell the Administration they had gone too far. This Administration acted as if they were above the law. Karl Rove, author of the plan to use DOJ to attack local level Democrats, remains in contempt of Congress. Today, everyone who cares about their vanishing civil liberties and freedoms needs to be concerned.

Why the hell are we here?

Weeks after the trail, one of the jurors called Jerry Crawford to ask why a mistrial wasn't called as it was obvious after the opening statements that a case didn't exist. That a juror would contact Crawford following a trial has happened only two or three times in all the years he's been a defense attorney. The juror had continually worried about this, thus needed to get it off their mind. The juror shared with Crawford that during their first break, one of the jurors entered the jury room, slammed their yellow pad on the table asking, "Why the hell are we here?!"

Why did I prevail?

I believed I prevailed because:
Falsely charged
Outstanding attorneys
Truth was on my side
FBI worked from false premises
FBI having to create a "crime" to investigate
Good private investigators
FBI's chief witness was my best witness
"Facts" created by the prosecution simply were not logical
Questionable practices by federal attorneys and FBI
Questionable actions within the grand jury

Cost was a waste of taxpayer's money

The attitude of win at any cost became the modus operandi of the DOJ. What should have been a minuscule case was blown into a major court battle. The $1,800 paid to me by Vasquez for my commissions would not have even risen to the level of District Court since the amount involved was about the threshold for small claims court.

The cost of this prosecution was disproportionate to the "crime." At least six FBI agents were involved by the prosecution, along with the Des Moines Chief of Police, a police lieutenant, as well as the Polk County Attorney's Office. On the federal payroll were Luxa, her boss Kevin Kohler and Ann Brickley, who was flown in from the Department of Public Integrity in Washington, D.C. Brickley probably made a dozen trips in and out of Des Moines preparing for my trial. Prosecutor Lester Paff also had to be paid. We cannot forget those directly linked to the courtroom. Two judges, their staffs, and the court stenographers were part of the cost of this sham. Not transparent was their massive support staff working behind the scenes. This colossal prosecution team pitched a major large-scale operation activated by $1,800–less than what Vasquez was paid to trap me. But, Whitaker told the press there were no political motivations behind this case. Clearly, the evidence would suggest otherwise.

Government should compensate McCoy for legal fees

January 17, 2008--Gil Cranberg in a *Cityview* Guest Commentary wrote: "Why did the government press a case so thin it bordered on the anorexic? It's not that public corruption is a particular priority of the U.S. Attorney Matt Whitaker. Asked about his priorities during a radio interview at the time McCoy was indicted, Whitaker made no mention of public corruption. Yet his office had the FBI and at least four prosecutors, including one sent especially from Washington, in pursuit of a case that appeared to be no more than a falling out over a petty business deal. Along the way, prosecutors misled McCoy's lawyers for months about the payments it made to win the cooperation of the government's chief witness...the government caused McCoy and his family enormous pain. Jurors did their part to ease the pain, but when the government mounts as flimsy a case as it did against McCoy, there ought to be a way to compensate such victims for their legal defense.

The Justice Department supposedly subjects the cases it brings to careful prior review in Washington. If the department is unwilling to disclose who OK'd the McCoy prosecution, and why, Congress ought to step in and demand answers. A top-to-bottom review ought to include how and why the case came to the attention of the U.S. Attorney and the nature of the evidence presented to the grand jury."[64]

Kibbie view of impact of trial

Kibbie thought the trial and everything I went through "helped Matt become a stronger and better legislator, a more resolved legislator, a more engaged legislator to prove to himself something. In the Legislative session following his trial he was really into the issues. Very few people in the session could handle the legislation any better than or as well as he did. He did his homework. Staff helped but he still had to be the messenger. The legislative session following his trial was a positive thing for him–he was out in public meeting people, giving speeches. I think he had more confidence and is surer of himself. Our Caucus would be unified in saying this. Matt knew when to compromise on issues and get a little at a time and that we needed to get the caucus re-elected. If he isn't at the top in that legislative session, he'd be near the top."

Disturbing potshots from Paff

Paff's most disturbing potshot targeted at me was when he had implied that I had misused my position. He implied that I knew where development in the downtown areas were headed and I was able to acquire attractive properties in those areas. Then, he took another direct hit, "Will there ever be enough money for you? Is there ever enough money?" That ticked me off because there was a lot of risk whenever I purchased property. I didn't think the question "was there ever enough money for you?" was worth an answer.

How my life changed as a result of the trial

The trial has changed my life in a lot of ways. I'm more cautious with whom I talk and what I say. I'm certainly more cautious with whom I get involved in with business. And, I'm more realistic about my country and the activities of my government. I love my country, I just happen to have a lot of concerns about our current government. I would be the first to question the facts they present. My finances have changed. I have had a difficult time as a result of all the cash that went out to defend myself.

I am reminded of the things that matter in life are family, friendships, and freedom. Things acquired are of little value.

I am in a position now where I don't feel tied up in knots, I am able to eat, able to laugh, able to enjoy life, and that's very positive thing. But, I am also always looking over my shoulder for the next shoe to drop.

Loss of clients and potential income

What happened to me when my business associates and colleagues were confronted by the FBI because of me? There is residue when something so traumatic like that happens. It is a fear process. Attorneys for one of my clients distanced my client from me advising our business relationship be terminated. My relationship with another client of five years, with whom I was helping broker real estate sales, for all respects ended. The opportunity cost to me was high that resulted from the FBI's quest to make me a criminal. It also cost me a seat or chair of an important legislative committee. Also gone, was an assistant leadership position inside my own Caucus made up of all the Democratic Senators.

Surviving challenges

Many of us have struggled with paradoxes. You may identify with mine:

Being born into a strong, close Catholic family with supportive caring parents, yet unable to confide in them my darkest secrets leaving me to cope in isolation.

Marrying a loving, intelligent, successful wife with a beautiful baby, yet plagued by uncontrollable attraction toward men creating fearful panic of being exposed and self-loathing.

Managing successful business and political careers each accompanied with a wide network of associates and admiring friends, yet feeling alone weighted down fearing a Richard Cory[65] syndrome.

Having over-reported to the State of Iowa in total transparency business financials with the State, yet charged for extortion by U.S. Attorney Matt Whitaker and the U.S. Department of Justice.

Enduring nine agonizing days of an expensive trial, yet the jury took only 25 minutes to find me not guilty.

Thinking the attack on me by the DOJ was an isolated incident, yet later learning it was part of a series of charges by the DOJ on leading Democrats at the grassroots level.

If you are experiencing challenges, be assured you are not alone in dealing with difficulties. You, too, can survive what seems like insurmountable circumstances.

November 2018--Won seat on Polk County Board of Supervisors

In 2018, I announced that I would seek a seat on the Polk County Board of Supervisors. I was elected with 82% of the vote against John Mauro who had held the seat for many years.

The opportunity to serve in an elective office has been a high honor for which I am grateful. I will continue to stand for equality, transparency, and justice reform. I will continue to be a voice for the under-represented, the marginalized, and for a strong middle class.

Mom knows we'll find the answer someday

When mother was asked by a friend if we'd ever find out the truth why the government pursued this case, my mother reassured her friend, "Yes, when we go to heaven." Puzzled her friend searched for meaning in her answer. "Well you know the saying, 'Only God knows' so he'll let us know when we get there."

We must speak out. It is our duty. In the words of Ben Franklin, "They that can give up essential liberty to obtain a little temporary safety deserve neither liberty nor safety.

Appendices

Appendix A: *POLITICO Magazine*, "I was the Subject of a Political 'Witch Hunt,' Matt Whitaker Directed It," by Matt McCoy, November 11, 2018

Appendix B: CNN Interview, "Whitaker's controversial prosecution of a gay Democrat," by Drew Griffin, Collette Richards and Patricia DiCarlo, November 8, 2018

Appendix C: Blogs, *The Des Moines Register*, 2007

Appendix D: *The Des Moines Register*, "Letter to the Editor," May 29, 2018 (Letter in support of my candidacy for Polk County Supervisor citing my legacy from years serving in the Iowa State Senate)

Appendix E: Awards and Recognitions

Appendix F: Acknowledgements

Appendix G: Authors

Appendix H: Sources Cited

Appendix A: POLITICO

Politico Magazine

I was the Subject of a Political 'Witch Hunt.' Matt Whitaker Directed it. By Matt McCoy

Trump's interim pick for AG was part of an investigation that was covered in partisan fingerprints.

Matt McCoy is a state senator from Iowa's 21st District. November 11, 2018

On the morning of April 7, 2006, two FBI agents knocked on my door. They informed me that I was being investigated about issues related to bribery and violation of the Hobbs Act. As I tried to recall what the Hobbs Act entailed (robbery and extortion, mostly), they prolonged their visit by pressing "play" on a tape recorder. I was shocked to hear a conversation I had conducted with my business colleague, Tom Vasquez.

That conversation detailed a dispute we had, regarding my consulting with Vasquez about a business that sold monitoring systems for senior citizens in Iowa. The federal government believed that in my demanding payment for those services, and threatening to strike out on my own as a competitor, I had made what amounted to a threat to use the power of my office against him.

The FBI claimed this threat was extortion by an elected Iowa state senator. I explained how I had filed the required Senate financial disclosure forms, and that, as citizen legislators who work in the capital for less than one-third of the year, we have to have other employment, hence this dispute. They disagreed, arguing that my comments amounted to an attempt to coerce Vasquez. The *Des Moines Register* reported during my eventual trial that numerous Iowa officials had "denied threats by McCoy, and insisted that no single senator would have the power to influence purchasing decisions" by the state.

However, not satisfied with snaring just me in their net, the agents went on to say that if I gave them the names of other elected officials engaged in illegal activities, the district court might be inclined to look favorably on me. The district office was led by a prosecutor named Matt Whitaker, then the U.S. attorney for the Southern District of Iowa. Whitaker, an avowed conservative who has run for state office multiple times as a Republican, was part of what would come to be widely considered a politically motivated effort by the Department of Justice to investigate Democratic officeholders.

At the time, David Yepsen of the *Register* wrote: "It appears the U.S. attorney, Matt Whitaker, is aggressively going after the city's south-side Democratic organization and the way it does business." You could call it due diligence, and, to be clear, the investigation and secret recording of my conversations was done in a fully legal manner. But if you consider Whitaker's naked partisanship, as Yepsen did, and the fact that a study at the time showed that the Ashcroft and Gonzales Departments of Justice prosecuted Democrats to an extent grossly disproportionate to Republicans, you could refer to it as something very different. In Whitaker's own recent words: a "witch hunt."

The FBI agents who visited me that day were saying that if I snitched on my Senate colleagues, Whitaker's office might be lenient with me. This is all standard practice for the Department of Justice, of course, and similar to the tactics that special counsel Robert Mueller, who Whitaker has repeatedly criticized, has used in his ongoing investigation—but ignoring the fact that I had no knowledge of what I was supposed to have done illegally, let alone knowledge of illegal actions on the part of others, I would never have played that game.

This was the first I knew I was under federal scrutiny. The FBI paid Vasquez to record 12 hours of our conversations. They turned over the tapes to the grand jury. The jury returned a one-count indictment against me for attempted extortion under the Hobbs Act, which more specifically is a federal anti-racketeering law used in cases involving public corruption. It sets a low bar for conviction of public officials. The charge stemmed from the threat to form my own company. The FBI admitted to paying at least $2,200 to Vasquez for clandestinely taping our conversations. If I were convicted, it could have meant a $250,000 fine and 20 years imprisonment.

Whitaker's entire case was built on the word of Vasquez, the star witness, whose credibility was undermined by a litany of personal issues he acknowledged under oath. In cross-examination,

Vasquez had amnesia. "I can't recall," "I don't remember" was his response to over 100 questions.

That the FBI paid Vasquez for his testimony was unheard of. The former editor of *The Des Moines Register*'s editorial page, Gilbert Cranberg, stated, "The local criminal defense bar was stunned that the government had to pay the alleged victim for his help prosecuting his purported victimizer," in an editorial for the *Nieman Watchdog*. In a local news journal, he wrote: "Was McCoy's prosecution a product of poor judgment, inexperience, misplaced zeal or partisan politicking? Perhaps some or all of the above."

I was eventually acquitted after the jury deliberated for less than 25 minutes, according to the foreman. Cranberg noted in the *Register*, "The case against McCoy was so anorexic that not one of the 12 jurors considered it worth protracted consideration." One of my attorneys, Montgomery Brown, stated, "Ninety percent of federal court cases result in a conviction, and the swift 'not guilty' verdict indicates something was seriously wrong with Whitaker's case."

U.S. attorneys conveniently "forgot" that they approved to pay Vasquez to covertly tape his conversations with me, a revelation that came out in the wind-up to my trial. There were no consequences for this. In denying our motion to dismiss the case, the court said this was an unfortunate "lapse of memory." Had I had such a lapse, I would have been cuffed and hauled off to prison.

According to my attorney, Jerry Crawford, during the trial he walked over to the prosecuting attorneys and asked them to save face, saying, "Pull this case now. I'm embarrassed for the United States of America." Both of the attorneys he spoke to, one of whom had been flown in from Washington, D.C., by the DOJ, said they were instructed to carry out the case to its fullest extent. Somebody in Washington—or in Whitaker's office—was making this call, and the trial prosecutors didn't have control over it. They knew they were out-lawyered, and they were getting slaughtered daily in court. But they couldn't bring it to a close, which would have saved them both money and time.

Whitaker's office clearly wanted to give the evangelical right within the Republican Party a trophy, and that trophy was me— one of the state's most prominent young Democrats at the time.

Whitaker is a social conservative who supported the Iowa Christian Alliance, the pre-eminent group in the state for like-minded conservatives. In 2014, he was executive director of the Foundation for Accountability and Civil Trust (FACT), a conservative watchdog, which *Slate* described as a "Dark Money-Funded Clinton Antagonist...[which] largely publicized what it described as ethical lapses by prominent Democrats and requested that government agencies and law enforcement investigate them."

People should be very concerned with Whitaker's elevation to acting attorney general. The DOJ is supposed to be blind to politics. Whitaker clearly is not.

At the time, I did not realize the full implications of what was happening to me, which had echoes in national politics. The U.S. attorney general at the time, Alberto Gonzales, was involved in a scandal in which he was accused of firing eight U.S. prosecutors, who were all previously in good standing with the DOJ, for political reasons. The aforementioned study from the time suggests the DOJ was attacking the Democratic Party at its grass roots.

Their insinuations of corruption sapped local Democrats of energy and created suspicion among their constituents.

At the time, the national Democratic Party had named me among the 100 up-and-coming Democratic leaders to watch. I was young. I was liberal. I was popular. I had never been defeated. I had flirted with running for Congress. And I was openly gay, which surely didn't increase my popularity with social conservatives like Whitaker. Steve Deace, the conservative talk radio host, hosted Whitaker on his show in 2007 and referred to me derogatorily as "openly homo." Whitaker said nothing, aside from protesting in favor of his impartiality. He said to Deace that he was "personally offended" by such accusations of partisanship, and that he "[didn't] have time to direct investigations that I'm not specifically working on myself."

Whitaker has attempted to establish his own career in Iowa politics. He lost a run for state treasurer in 2002, lost a Republican primary bid for the U.S. Senate in 2014, and was not selected for a seat on the Iowa Supreme Court despite angling for the job. It's hard to believe he could carry out the important job of United States attorney general with a sense of fealty to the law and to the Constitution, rather than to the Republican Party.

The government's invasion of my privacy during the case Whitaker's office brought against me was hardly unusual for such an investigation, but considering my innocence and exculpation it was appalling: I was followed, my conversations were recorded, and my financial records were seized. Family members, co-workers, legislative colleagues and acquaintances were questioned. My emails were read. The emails and financial records of a business colleague were subpoenaed. My reputation and future were damaged. The emotional stress took its toll on my physical and mental health. I lost both actual and potential income, along with my savings. When the DOJ wields its power in a partisan manner, it ruins lives. Whitaker almost ruined mine.

I left in debt, and with and a shattered sense of security. Whitaker left noting his "complete confidence in the jury system."

Hopefully that confidence endures to this day, regardless of what such a jury might have to say about his new benefactor.

Appendix B: CNN Interview

CNN

Whitaker's controversial prosecution of a gay Democrat
By Drew Griffin, Collette Richards and Patricia DiCarlo, CNN

Updated 11:25 PM ET, Fri November 9, 2018

(CNN) When Iowa state Sen. Matt McCoy learned Donald Trump had appointed Matthew Whitaker to be acting attorney general of the United States, he was aghast--he believes Whitaker was behind a politically motivated prosecution that was personally "devastating" to him.

It started in 2007, when McCoy was a rising Democrat in state politics, and the state's first openly gay lawmaker. Whitaker was the US attorney for Iowa's Southern District at the time.

A grand jury indictment accused McCoy of using his elected office to try to extort $2,000 from a Des Moines home security company where McCoy was a consultant. The charges came after an elaborate undercover investigation in which the FBI had McCoy's business partner wear a recording device. McCoy demanded money he says he was owed for his consulting work.

In an interview with CNN this week, McCoy said Whitaker "certainly tried to prove that I had done something really awful when, in fact, it was a garden variety business dispute that should have been handled in small claims court, if anywhere."

Whitaker said he supports state's rights to nullify federal law

The trial lasted more than a week, with prosecutors trying to prove the business partner never agreed to pay McCoy for his consulting and the defense torpedoing the partner's testimony because he couldn't recall many details and admitted he had trouble with sobriety, according to Des Moines Register articles on the trial.

In the end, the jury reached a not guilty verdict in an hour and a half, including time for lunch, according to the Des Moines Register.

"I believe it was a political prosecution, there's no doubt in mind, I'm 100% certain that it was," McCoy said, adding he believes he was targeted not just because he's a Democrat, but also because he's gay. "As US attorney (Whitaker) spoke at Christian Coalition events and would often refer to bringing God into his decision-making process and being guided by God's hand," McCoy said, "and so I believe that he was very much resentful of my lifestyle and I believe that played a factor in it."

Whitaker has been facing questions from reporters about whether the case was politically motivated since the day the indictment was announced in 2007. An editorial in the Des Moines Register soon after McCoy was acquitted called for the government to compensate McCoy for his legal fees and questioned, "Was the McCoy prosecution a product of poor judgment, inexperience, misplaced zeal or partisan politicking? Perhaps all of the above."

A Justice Department official sent a statement to CNN defending the case. "As a U.S. Attorney, then–US Attorney Whitaker had a responsibility to uphold the rule of law and pursue credible allegations of illegal activity. The Department of Justice signed off on bringing the case, the FBI conducted an independent investigation, and career prosecutors handled the case throughout its duration. The jury's verdict does not negate the obligation of law enforcement agencies to open cases when they determine laws may have been broken."

Whitaker ran conservative group funded by dark money

McCoy said the two-year legal battle exhausted his finances and left a lasting impact on his life. "I was putting my whole family in an emotional state as a result of that. I had elderly parents, I had a young son...It took an emotional toll on the people that I loved and it was completely unnecessary."

McCoy continued as a state senator for 11 more years, a position he will hold until January. He was just elected to the Polk County Board of Supervisors, winning with 82% of the vote.

Whitaker left his position as US attorney in 2009 and ran unsuccessfully for the US Senate in 2014. He also unsuccessfully vied for a seat on the Iowa Supreme Court, then went on to create the Foundation for Accountability and Civic Trust, a Washington nonprofit funded almost entirely by dark money. In 2017, he became former Attorney General Jeff Sessions' chief of staff until this week, when he stepped into his former boss' job.

CNN's Scott Bronstein and Madeleine Ayer contributed to this report.

Appendix C: Blogs

The Des Moines Register Blogs

Bloggers had a field day playing Monday Morning Quarterbacks over my trial. "The Des Moines Register" was the site of choice. Bloggers, of course, remain anonymous. Consequently, they are not held accountable for their bluntness. We were able to discern the identity of one of the bloggers–blondebutnotdumb. During the trial she sat among my family or next to Ferguson, even following him into the hallway in an attempt to overhear his telephone conversation that pertained to my trial. My mother caught on to her game and warned the rest of us to be careful with what we told her. It was the "Loose lips sink ships" scenario and mom did not want my ship to sink. I pulled these blogs from the "The Des Moines Register." The sampling was simply what was there. I did not attempt to stack the deck. Whitaker is often mentioned. His name is printed in bold print as he was key to what happened to me. Blogs are presented as written.

Blogs

March 15, 2007

Brindee wrote:

Why did Vasquez receive payments from the government this past August & September? This came out in today's hearing. What else is the government hiding? Caesar had Brutus. McCoy had Vasquez. Betrayal behavior doesn't change. It will be interesting to see how many others have been victims of Vasquez's "friendship."

October 20, 2007

Richard wrote:

Read the last paragraph. I have no opinion about McCoy's guilt or innocence in this matter. But, for him to out someone for being in AA, especially after that person "offered to help McCoy with his own sobriety" is the lowest of the low. Just what does McCoy not understand about "anonymous"????? McCoy is a snake in the grass, but so-called liberals in WDM (*West Des Moines*) keep electing him. Why? We know the answer.

McCoy's betrayal of a fellow alcoholic NO MATTER WHAT THE CIRCUMSTANCES is a violation of trust. If he can betray this trust, why would anyone trust him to be an elected representative? I don't know. Ask the WDM voters. They keep doing it.

October 20, 2007

RevGreen wrote:

so it's not a stereotype that politicians are all alcoholics this whole case is right wing CONspiracy from the neo coms.

October 20, 2007

Brindee wrote:

Had Richard read the 8 page statement McCoy submitted to the *Register* he would have realized that he didn't out anyone. McCoy was simply explaining how it came about that he befriended the guy who secretly taped their conversations. It was a basic explanation that was needed. The betrayal here was Vasquez betraying McCoy who had tried to help him.

October 20, 2007

Richard wrote:

McCoy was simply explaining how it came about that he befriended the guy who secretly taped their conversations.

And just how is that not outing him? Nice try, but it doesn't work. There are other ways to explain how you met someone than by saying "through AA." That's betrayal of trust and confidentiality any way you want to spin it. What is it about anonymity that YOU don't understand Brindee?

The lengths some people will go to defend the undefendable is amazing. If McCoy's attorneys want to question a person's past alcohol and drug use, especially if that person is in recovery, then they must be desperate.

October 20, 2007

The Fonz wrote:

AA is a cult just like the Moonies or the hara Krishnas. There's no confidentiality expected when you break away from the cult.

October 20, 2007

Brindee wrote:

Richard–Oh yes, I do understand. My comments were more than "a nice try," they probably are the truth. I agree with you that this is a major violation of trust, confidentiality, and anonymity. However, it appears that McCoy is Vasquez's victim here. Vasquez is the one that violated McCoy's trust, etc. Richard how would you react if you were McCoy and a trusted friend violated your bond of friendship (AA etc.) through 12 hours of undercover taping? Authorities would want to know why you were friends and you would have to acknowledge you were AA brothers because the trust had already been violated.

October 20, 2007
Richard wrote:
AA is a cult just like the Moonies or the hara Krishnas.
Spoken like a true drunk.

October 23, 2007
ddelly wrote:
The government responded Tuesday urging Gritzner not to postpone the trial, citing the lineup of witnesses prepared to testify and the potential for media coverage to affect the jury pool. = so the judge thought the gov prosecutor was wrong and granted the defense's motion = I don't know how the tapes will change from now until then. Are the witnesses in a federal protection program? was the fbi wrong?

October 23, 2007
RevGreen wrote:
And how much were the informants paid

November 3, 2007
Brindee wrote:
Gilbert Cranberg's article reflects an indepth understanding of our current political scene. He obviously has followed the flow of the Gonzales Department of Injustice's attacks on Democrats at the local level.

The gross abuse of power in this case has been done by the Dept. of Justice and the FBI. It is scary when United States Attorneys lie to manufacture a case. It is an abysmal misuse of power in a democracy to allow the government of spy on its civilians. History is full of such acts--including bribing one citizen to spy on another. Being a paid snitch is hardly the same as doing one's patriotic duty.

The defense has not filed repeated motions for dismissal. This is the first motion for dismissal. It was done--as clearly reported in the Register--because the U.S. Attorney's had lied to the defense in writing causing them to have to re-think their entire case to try to ascertain where the U.S. government lied to them and when they were told the truth. The Judge at the Motion for Continuance Hearing called the prosecutor's case a "moving target".

December 5, 2007

Perfectiming wrote:

McCoy's words will clear, not convict him. And, it's not one person's words against him. It's a political system out to undermine Democrats at the local level--read the national news and connect the dots. McCoy's words say, "Let's just part friends, you keep your check, I do not want your money. I'll compete with you in business." He told Vasquez who betrayed him, "Tom I don't want you to get hurt. I want to help you."

Vesquez placed over 200 telephone calls to McCoy -- hardly someone worried about being extorted.

December 5, 2007

Brindee wrote:

We need to know how much the government has spent trying to trap McCoy. Some estimate $750,000--others close to $1,000,000. And what in the world has it cost McCoy? Gonzales was in dsm talking with **Whitaker** in the final hours of his term as Attorney General. Did they discuss McCoy? Is **Whitaker** using this as a stepping stone to run for governor?

December 5, 2007

Brindee wrote:

Matt McCoy's trail is demonstrating how badly our civil liberties have been abused. The government's star witness testified that he lied to the grand jury as well as to the FBI. The U.S. Attorney lied in writing to McCoy's defense lawyers. She forgot four times that she approved payment to McCoy's friend to covertly tape conversations with him because he feared he was being by-passed in a business deal. Did those lies cause the grand jury to indict McCoy?

Prior to offering McCoy a business offer, he offered several other people.

The government's star witness took the Gonzales approach stating 87 times today in court that he "couldn't remember" when asked questions.

Innocent citizens--like McCoy--are having their entire life destroyed by those seeking to enhance their own careers or political careers.

December 6, 2007
Brindee wrote:

The Federal Government's star witness Tom Vasquez reviewed his record of payments by the FBI (the very ones they lied in writing about) and acknowledged that he was paid $150 for a 15 minute phone conversation with McCoy. Looks like McCoy wasn't the only one being duped.

An ex-girlfriend of Vasquez testified that she loaned him $3,000 which he never repaid. She also testified that after Tom realized he was not going to be an important part of the new business deal with McCoy, he said he was going to hurt McCoy, it was going to be big, it would be in the news, he would be the one responsible for it, and that he was going to do it through Des Moines Detective Terry Mitchell.

December 7, 2007
Brindee wrote:

Prosecutors in the McCoy trail continue to manufacture their bogus case. They attempted to say McCoy did not file his Senate financial and ethic forms in a timely manner. Apparently they forgot the testimony of their own witnesses (Pres. of Senate Jack Kibby, & Senate legal committee Steve Conway) who both state McCoy had over disclosed. Both made it clear that Senators have a right to sell products to the state and McCoy was within his rights to do so.

Prosecutors played a secretly made tape of McCoy in his office on Dec. 21 2005 with Tom Vasquez and his boss Reid Schultz. McCoy clearly stated that he didn't want to do business with them, they could keep their $500 check (which they took w/them) for the work he had completed, and they would part friends. McCoy even gave Vasquez a hug -- which made a "pounding" sound as McCoy pressed against Tom's hidden recorder.

Picture that scene. A friend hugs his Judas causing Judas' hidden recorder of betrayal to record the scene.

December 13, 2007

OhKaye wrote:

Shame on the arrogant naysayers who think they know more than the jurors! Matt McCoy was acquitted because he is INNOCENT. If you relied simply on news coverage to form an opinion, you certainly don't have all the facts. The jurors, on the other hand, heard days of testimony at great disruption to their own lives to render a fair and impartial verdict. Matt McCoy was always innocents – that's how our justice systems works – innocent until PROVED otherwise. The jury has spoken. Mr. McCoy REMAINS INNOCENT.

December 13, 2007

Brindee wrote:

Blondebutnotdumb – you seem to be launching a lot of unfair attacks on the McCoy family. Is that because early on in the trail they figured out who you are?

December 13, 2007

Rugby wrote:

Jury out 2 hours? Have a bite, go the restroom, elect a foreperson, read thru the jury instructions once, vote once, unanimous, then wait a few little so does not look like your hurried. Then deliver a legal ass-whopping to the Feds. A 2-hour verdict means "no case."

December 13, 2007

Blondbutnotdum wrote:

Nobody is talking about the skillful lawyering of Monty Brown, who singlehandedly won the case! He is a brilliant attorney. This was not politically motivated prosecution, and you would know that if you sat through the entire trial. It was about great lawyering and nothing more!

December 13, 2007

Brindee wrote:

The McCoy case has "politics" written all over it. Gonzales spent his final hours in office with **Whittaker**. The Department of Justice has been going after Democratic officials at the local level. Did Mitchell and Vasquez provide the unfounded "justification" for the FBI to go after yet another local level Democrat? Let's get those dots connected.

December 13, 2007

Bubba wrote:

I doubt it was politically motivated, and I only know what I saw in the *Register* and TV, but I had a feeling all along this case should never have been taken to trial. I just hope that Matt McCoy can pay his legal fees and keep on doing the good work.

December 13, 2007

Ervserver wrote:

No surprise with this verdict, the case wasn't even close to being proved. **The prosecutor who pursued this case should be reprimanded.**

December 13, 2007

SDMNative wrote:

Will the *Register* please investigate the U.S. Attorney's office so that we can learn how the prosecutors "forgot" that the FBI had paid a informant to help it manufacture a case against McCoy? The Register seemed to relish the idea of a politician on trial, and the real abuse was not sufficiently exposed. Now that McCoy has been vindicated, I hope the media will do its job and scrutinize the conduct of the Bush/Gonzales Justice Department.

December 13, 2007

Josyph wrote:

As someone who watched a great deal of this trial, I must say that the jury made the right decision. Not only was there a great deal of reasonable doubt—there was confidence that he was completely innocent by the end of the trial. Matt McCoy has always been a great Senator and I hope this ridiculous excuse for a trial doesn't set him back. I agree, **Whitaker** should resign.

December 13, 2007
Exiowan wrote:

Whitaker was in my law school class. I can honestly say he does not represent the class well. shame, shame.

December 13, 2007
Mr Jimi wrote:

This sure looks like a politically motivated prosecution by **Whitaker** to please his bosses in the Bush Administration.

December 13, 2007
Prezelman wrote:

Always knew McCoy was innocent…he's always been a stand up guy. Govt. was sent on **political witch hunt**

December 13, 2007
Jack DM wrote:

Did I call it, or did I call it? ☺ WHEN will the Republicans learn that politically motivated prosecutions just won't work? It didn't work for Nixon, Reagan, and Bush 1. Hopefully this will start sending a message to Justice that Bush 2 doesn't have a crown and scepter.

December 13, 2007
Irish Jim wrote:

Glad to see so many others sharing my sentiments. This was an enormous waste of taxpayer money and time. I hope **Whitaker** will follow suit of his former boss Alberto Gonzales and resign to spend more time with his family.

December 13, 2007
Romofo wrote:

Not guilty? What a lame excuse for a jury.

December 13, 2007
Mano26 wrote:

Over $2,000? Go find a real case to make an example of! This was a waste of time and money.

December 13, 2007
Finally wrote:

How do you spell it. . .V I N D I C A T I O N!

December 13, 2007
WDMBOB wrote:

Now someone should investigate Mr. **Whitaker's** motivations for moving forward with this flimsy case.

December 13, 2007
Payyalater wrote:

The FBI paid Vasquez more $ to wear a wire than this whole case is about. Why don't they go find some bad guys?

December 13, 2007
OhKaye wrote:

Romofo--were you present during the hours and hours of testimony? Did you hear all the evidence heard by the jury? I don't think so. You owe the jurors an apology. Those who followed the trial day in and day out came to the same conclusion as the jury--Matt McCoy is INNOCENT. How dare anyone question the hard work and decision making made by the 12 women and men whose lives were disrupted so that justice could be served. We owe them a huge thanks for their service. No matter our opinion, my opinion, or anyone else's opinion--Matt McCoy is innocent in the eyes of our justice system. The jury has spoken.

December 14, 2007
Brindee wrote:

The jury saw through all the lies told by the government's chief witness as well as by the U.S. Attorneys and the FBI. This should have been stopped by Mitchell's supervisors at the Des Moines Police Department or our County Attorney's office. Why did any thinking individual allow these trumped up charges to move forward? This has been a tremendous cost to taxpayers as well as to McCoy. Can Vasquez be held responsible for any of this? Testimony in court included statements that Vasquez has left a trail of human destruction in his path. The FBI rushed to find "evidence" to prove they were right in wanting to believe McCoy did something wrong. Maybe this trial will help restore some of the damage that has been done by the Dept. of Justice. Who will hold the FBI agents accountable?

December 14, 2007

Rockodsm wrote:

Great verdict. It was a thin case that should not have gone this far. Someone's political agenda could have cost this man 20 years inside. *The Des Moines Register* does its level best to make a villain out of everyone that is arrested. Case in point "listen to the audio recording" at the top of the page. After the verdict is read they still want people to think bad of this man. Fortunately, he has not lost 20 years of his life. Unfortunately, he has probably spent $50-$100,000 on attorney expense. I think there should be an avenue for him to recover this from the feds. But they don't care, no one is responsible for that.

December 14, 2007

Fanomite wrote:

I COULD NOT WAIT!!! to comment on this article. I really want to go back and find the earlier stories about this and rehash what some of you wrote about how guilty McCoy was. God how I love to see you eat Crow! First, let me congratulate Mr. McCoy and his defense team. I wish I could buy you guys dinner and I will if I ever see you out and about! Thank you a thousand times for slapping the snot out of the smartasses that use scum like the snitch that Agent Kohlers used. Remember this case, this is the one where Kohlers and his buddies tried to do a frame-up on McCoy by snipping 14 hours out of 15 hours of recordings. The **US Attorney's** office and FBI lied about paying the snitch. They have spent THOUSANDS of our tx dollars. I'll give you my pitch. THEY should be prosecuted. They are NOT held responsible by anybody. They get away with this crap every day. Eat crow those of you who had this man in prison. Eat it good!

December 14, 2007

Emptygee wrote:

Justice has been upheld, and I'm glad to hear it. Meanwhile, the CIETC crew walks the streets...Great appropriation of our prosecutorial resources!!

December 14, 2007

IMME56 wrote:

6thof90f11 Obviously you have information that should have been shared with the jury, a group of 12 who heard all the evidence and not one of them felt McCoy was guilty and it only took an hour and a half for them to make that decision. From all appearances it would be much more likely that the Republican appointed **Fed District Attorney** was a pursuing a **political agenda** against a Democratic politician.

December 14, 2007

Hemroid wrote:

What a waste of tax payer's money over a lousy $2,000, what 2 tanks of gas?

December 14, 2007

Blondbutnotdumb, I did sit through a great deal of the trial. It was a pathetically weak case. Yes, the lawyering was good, and praise should go to Mr. Brown. However, the case brought by the government was just not there. Why would the government bring a case with no convincing evidence? Well, the only reason I can think of is they had a **political motivation** (which is easy to believe given the numerous scandals of the justice department as of late).

December 14, 2007

Blondebutnot dumb wrote

By the way, Rich Eychaner, is a well-known "Republican" who sat through most of the Trial... wonder what he thinks...being a Republican and all?

December 14, 2007

Blondebutnotdumb wrote:

And by knowing who I am, do you mean a member of the General Public at a Public Trial? Speaking of unfair attacks and unsubstantiated assumptions...the McCoy family is certainly paranoid? Are they naturally suspicious or are they sure that everyone is out to get them?

December 14, 2007

Jamanau2 wrote:

It appears he skated on this one. I wonder if his "forgetting" to pay for the medicine at a grocery store will be a similar result?? Makes one wonder about the whole process?

December 14, 2007

Josysph wrote:

bbnd, I wouldn't attack your intelligence if you didn't use ridiculous arguments to go on attacking an innocent man. Testifying in a trial as a witness for one side or the other is not necessarily a reflection of one's affiliation. There is a system for compelling witnesses to testify. I heard many prosecution witnesses who testified about how clean Mr. McCoy's hands were in this matter. In fact, I would say most of the government's witnesses did more to prove McCoy's innocence than they did to prove his guilty. And just because the lawyers representing McCoy didn't go so far as to characterize this prosecution as politically motivated in the media doesn't mean it wasn't, and it doesn't even mean the lawyers didn't think so. In fact, Mr. Brown asked a rhetorical question in his closing arguments, alluding to his curiosity as to the real motivation behind this prosecution. I think that is an implicit charge against the government in this case.

December 14, 2007

3atm3 wrote:

He's got a lot of logos to buy....2,000 dollars worth....

December 14, 2007

Josyph wrote:

It was a pathetically weak case that never should have been brought to trial. For god sakes, the government paid the informant more money trying to manufacture evidence against McCoy than he had allegedly tried to extort...I agree that the *Register* seriously needs to look into the **US attorney's office**. The politics surrounding this targeted prosecution need to be exposed, and **Whitaker** needs to be exposed. Obviously this justice department won't hold him accountable, but maybe the people can.

December 14, 2007

dlmMac wrote:

It took the jury 2 hours, with a break for lunch, for a "Not Guilty" verdict. Maybe **Whitaker** should re-consider his long term political aspirations in Iowa, Governor, Senator etc.

December 14, 2007

Josyph wrote:

Blondbutnotdumb, your name is inaccurate. You may be blond, but the "not dumb" part, I'm not so sure. This jury acquitted McCoy in record time. it was not even close and they came to the right decision. I was watching this trial, and there was virtually no evidence against McCoy. The evidence put forward was insubstantial and completely unbelievable. So, given the fact that there was no evidence, **politics seems like the most likely motivation** for this prosecution. What is for sure is the motivation was not about finding the truth or doing justice. Shame on the **U.S. attorney's office.**

December 14, 2007

Blondebutnotdumb wrote:

Outside the courtroom, Brown and attorney Jerry Crawford later stopped just short of previous assertions that the case against McCoy, a Democrat, was **politically motivated.** I wonder why? Was it because there's no basis to it?

December 14, 2007

Blondebutnotdumb wrote:

Some of you uneducated dolts in dead end jobs with low wages.....need to seriously drink a better brand of Kool-Aid! The level of paranoia is unbelievable here! The McCoys think everyone is a spy who is out to get them. Some of you think this is part of a Vast Republican Conspiracy! More paranoia! The Government is out to get ALL Democrats! More paranoia!

December 14, 2007

Blondebutnotdumb wrote:

A NOT GUILTY verdict indicates that the evidence presented by the prosecutors may have indicated some level of guilt but not enough for THIS jury to convict him! Fanomite, are you heading up the Prosecution Team to go after FBI Agents and the **Department of Justice**? By the way, during those 11 hours of tapes, who was Senator McCoy working for? Feel free to pick more than one...but who was paying him during those times he was wasting time talking to Tom Vasquez? Just a question? 1. John Ruan 2. Team Development 3. Greater Des Moines Partnership 5. Personal Secrity Plus Inc. 6. Security Plus 7. State of Iowa?

December 14, 2007

Blondebutnotdumb wrote:

Former Alabama Governor Don Siegelman was charged Wednesday "in a 'widespread racketeering conspiracy' that includes allegations he took a bribe from former hospital executive Richard Scrushy for a key state appointment." Siegelman, who was governor from 1999 to 2003, was charged with racketeering, fraud, bribery, extortion and obstruction of justice. Siegelman called the long-running grand jury probe a political witch hunt by Republican prosecutors trying to derail his current Democratic campaign for a second term in 2006. "I never put a dime in my pocket that didn't belong there," he said Wednesday. Being affiliated with former Healthsouth CEO was pure as the driven snow!

December 14, 2007

Fanomite wrote:

Blonde said this: "The verdict by the jury does NOT indicate that Matt McCoy didn't do anything wrong, it's an indication that the jury didn't have enough evidence to convict him." LOL – you need to go back to civics class my dear. The jury doesn't have any evidence, they don't gather evidence and, contrary to popular opinion around here, the defendant is PRESUMED INNOCENT. This presumption stays with him until such time, if ever, the US proves his guilt beyond a reasonable doubt. In this case the US had to use trumped up, brought and paid for testimony of a pathological liar. Kohler and his crony buddies should be prosecuted for putting this man and his family through hell. Those prosecutors and FBI agents should be fired for gross incompetence. 9 days of trial. Hundreds of thousands of our dollars wasted. Makes me sick.

December 14, 2007

Blondebutnotdumb wrote:

Everything's political huh? This was one of those VAST REPUBLICAN CONSPIRACIES right? The Republicans had a pow-wow and they engaged Senator Kibbie, Kevin Concannon, DHS, AA, and countless others who ALL worked together to engage in an unprovoked witch hunt? That sounds reasonable to me!

December 14, 2007

JEP07 wrote:

What a waste of taxpayer time and money. Like Siegelman in Alabama, McCoy was the target of one of the most political administrations in history, that made political attack dogs one of our **Justice Department**. Like the pigs who took control the Doberman pups in "Animal Farm," our own Republican hog lot did the same with our prosecutors and their legal minions, and set them on a course they thought would assure their continued power for decades. So what happened in November 2006? Much, much more than Rove and the rest ever imagined. Real Justice? Someone should turn the same scrutiny against them.

December 14, 2007

Blondebutnotdumb wrote:

My family background related to the ownership of some radio stations, precludes me from EVER being picked for ANY jury, so you're safe iamwhoiam! I have a great profession which I enjoy but thanks for your unsolicited career advice iamwhoiam. My insights are my own perceptions about what I saw and heard, and are not the result of reading the few lame news accounts about this case. Some of the "characters" who were performing at the Federal Courthouse were a lot more interesting than I am. Should I name some names? Rich Eychaner, who runs an "interesting" Foundation. While I applaud his offering college scholarships, he keeps a helluva lot more than he gives out. Rich was appointed to the State Civil Rights Commission by Chet Culver, but it's a temporary appointment which the Republican members of the Iowa Legislature have voiced loud objections to Mr Eychaner. A vote on his appointment is upcoming.

December 14, 2007

Phreak 1983 wrote:

"The charge he faced was attempted extortion, rather than extortion because the money McCoy eventually received was provided by the FBI, not the former business partners." That's a load of crap! You don't get charged with attempting to sell drugs if you sell them to an FBI agent, so why is this not extortion?!

December 14, 2007

DukeMarinez wrote:

I knew this was a chicken shit case from the get go. People here in Iowa have no freakin clue what REAL extortion is. Live in New Jersey or Chicago a while and watch the local politicos in action there. This case wouldn't have made a blip on the radar.

December 14, 2007

Iamwhoiam wrote:

The glove did not fit - what could they do? What is going to happen to Thomas Vasquez? He is probably just beat up his girlfriend and is out smoking a bowl of marijuana right now trying to sell left over prescription drug on the street. Then he is heading over to the home of Reid Schultz to talk about the next person they can victimize. Come on Reid - it took you 18-months to find that business card? You testimony was less than believable. Shame on you for your lies.

December 14, 2007

Lumpenprole wrote:

They should arrest Brickley and charge her with being an idiot. Sometimes I wonder about the legal profession in this country. Alcoholics Anonymous would go out of business without the lawyers in this country. Google "drunken lawyer" and you will see what I mean.

December 14, 2007

IrishJim wrote:

JJCDAD, This jury did not acquit OJ. The fact that the US Attorneys office withheld the tape from the Grand Jury that had McCoy stating unequivocally that he would not sit here and extort and sacrifice his values over this deal, speaks volumes about what type of ethics **Matt Whitaker's** office has. He should be brought up on ethics charges with the State Bar Association. I hope someone files a malicious prosecution case against him. This was a complete waste of my tax dollars and **Whitaker** should be held accountable. If he has any sort of values whatsoever he would resign to spend more time with his family.

December 14, 2007
JUSTCUZ wrote:
Vasquez is a Snake! To all that put your faith in a con man, liar, cheat, thief,..shame on you. You should be embarrassed of yourself and hold on to whatever integrity you have left....If you have any left. How would you like to be in the next AA meeting with Vasquez? I bet there is a lot of open communication in that meeting. What happens to Vasquez? He should be held accountable somehow.

December 14, 2007
Pbjisms wrote:
thewholetruth I actually just went back through and read all the comments. You have been telling quite a few falsehoods yourself. The jurors requested to leave out a side exit and the majority of them did so. None of them fell asleep during the trial. I would consider yourself first before casting any additional stones.

December 14, 2007
Thewholetruth wrote:
There were at least 3 jurors who fell asleep during the Trial on several occasions. One juror listened to the entire Trial with his hands shoved in the pockets of his hooded sweatshirt as if he already knew the outcome. The two most educated jurors were alternates, who were excused at the end of the Trial, before the jury voted. To give you an idea of the impression the jury made...NONE Of the jurors portrayed themselves in any way other than, a bunch of lemmings even the way they were dressed. Nearly ALL of the male jurors wore hooded sweatshirts, ripped dirty jeans and a couple didn't even bother combing their hair. The women weren't much better with their faded jeans, one wore bedroom slippers, and flannel shirts that looked like they had seen better

days. Most of the jurors were chewing gum during the entire Trial process, which appeared not to be the case with ANY of the jurors with the exception of the 2 alternates.

December 14, 2007

Josyph wrote:

As far as what Mr. Eyechaner thinks, perhaps you should ask him. I bet he has his suspicions about the motivations behind this prosecution as well. As for the McCoy family, when you go into court and lie about who you are to them, of course they will regard you with suspicion. So, blonde, why don't you go back to the **U.S. Attorney's** office and go have some drinks with those people. You would probably get along well because you appear to have no grip on reality.

December 14, 2007

Matt Whitaker needs to resign. He did all of this for his own political agenda. If everyone does not recognize this they should. FBI agent Kohler needs to be fired for his lies on and off of the stand – I think that it is call perjury. US Assistant District Attorney Mary Luxa – should be disbarred for her lies. Her affiliation with Alcoholics Anonymous needs to be noted also. It is no longer a secret. Lester Paff is a puppet for the DOJ and the Southern District of Iowa – he should have known better. Ann Brickley needs to go back to DC and chase after some real criminals.

Iknowem wrote:

If a person can't extort a measly two grand, they have no business being in politics. What a novice. I'm ashamed of him.

Appendix D: Letter to Editor

Letter to the Editor of the *Des Moines Register*
Published: May 29, 2018
Dear Editor:

I have watched Matt McCoy stand on the Iowa State Senate floor speaking courageously on issues where others chose to remain silent. I have listened to him lead a highly complex budget proposal in the Senate with clarity, intelligence, and a carefully formulated rationale. I have observed him battling the Department of Human Services on behalf of the children in its system dying from willful neglect. And, I have watched the compassion with which he listened to a frantic father seeking support for his ill son and to the words of an anguished young man who felt he had been unfairly caught in the legal system. He listens and acts.

As I drive through the metro area I see the footprints of his legacy in the form of the new Central Iowa Shelter & Services, the revitalized Riverview Park, the mall on the west front of the Capitol where thousands now gather, the new DART Depot, improved facilities at the Easter Seals Camp, and improvements at the zoo.

The name "McCoy" is synonymous with "results." It is also synonymous with "compassion." Matt McCoy will bring these values to the Polk County Board of Supervisors.

Jim Ferguson
Clive, Iowa

Appendix E: Sen. Matt McCoy's Awards and Recognitions

Interal Jose Julio Sarria Civil Rights Award

Iowa Safe Schools Award

Woodrow Wilson Investing in Iowa's Highway Infrastructure

Friends of Fairs Award

Autism Society of Iowa Award

Primary Health Award

World Food Prize Leader

Iowa League of Cities

Foster Care Youth Council

2017 Legislator of the Year

Iowa Fraternal Alliance

Des Moines Area Regional Transit Authority

Iowa Hall of Fame Outstanding Elected Democrat

Easter Seals of Iowa National Legislative Leadership Award

Outstanding Service Award by Iowa Health Care Association and the Iowa Center for Assisted Living for his efforts to protect Iowa's elderly

Tai Dam Village Award

John F. Kennedy Award for Outstanding Leadership for Democratic Elected Official

Legislative Humanitarian Award - National Humane Society

Master Builders of Iowa

Des Moines Convention and Visitors Bureau Outstanding Legislator

Vision Iowa Legislative Leadership Award

First recipient of Central Iowa Shelter and Services Hero for the Homeless Award

Community HIV/Hepatitis Advocates of Iowa Network Legislative Award

Legislative Friend of Housing Award

Ducks Unlimited Public Policy Award

One Iowa's Sharon K. Malheiro Award for leadership on LGBT issues

Iowa Federation of the Blind Distinguished Service Iowa Award

Iowa Corn Growers Association Award

Autism Society of Iowa's Hometown Hero Award

First Class of the Des Moines *Business Record's* Forty under 40 Award recognizing young leaders in Des Moines

Victory Fund National Leadership Award

City View Favorite Bachelor (by vote of its readers)

Twice named by *City View* Favorite Legislator (by vote of its readers)

Harvard Study Award

Eagle Scout

Appendix F: Acknowledgements with Appreciation

For primary source interview:
  John Beamer
  Marc Beltrame
  F. Montgomery Brown
  Steve Conway
  Jerry Crawford
  Jeff Eckhoff
  Mike Gronstal
  Jack Kibbie
  Bill McCoy
  Mary McCoy
  Mike McCoy
  Jim Quilty
  Pam Whitmore
For consultation and support:
  Jim Autry
  Jill Ferguson
  Jennifer Heinz-Trow
  Greg Stieber
  Julia Williams
  Jonathan Wilson
For use of research document:
  Daniel Hoffman-Linnel

Appendix G: Authors
Matt McCoy

Matt McCoy was an Iowa State Senator and Iowa's highest ranking openly gay elected official. He has never lost election before or since coming out. He has served in the Iowa Legislature for twenty-six years, with key leadership roles in the Senate. Matt was a progressive voice in the Iowa Senate. He was an outspoken advocate for civil and human rights, and for children and vulnerable Iowans. McCoy was recognized as a defender of public education. In 2018 he was elected an Iowa Polk County Supervisor.

In 2007, he was charged with attempted extortion by the U.S. Department of Justice. U.S. Attorney General Alberto Gonzales and U.S. Attorney Matthew G. Whitaker led the prosecution. Following a nine-day jury trail, it took the jury only 25 minutes to find him not guilty. He agrees with the many journalists covering the case that it was politically motivated.

McCoy is co-author of <u>McCoy, You're Going Straight to Hell</u>. He is a graduate of Briar Cliff University. He and his son live in Des Moines, Iowa.

Matt McCoy   **Jim Ferguson**

Jim Ferguson

Jim Ferguson has served as a school administrator in Iowa, Texas and Michigan. The school where he served as principal was among the first to be recognized by the U.S. Department of Education as one of the most exemplary in the nation. He later taught at Simpson College. Ferguson worked with McCoy in the Senate and later in McCoy's firm, Resource Development Consultants. He co-authored a book with McCoy and is the author of numerous state and national publications. Ferguson earned his doctorate at The University of Iowa. He and his wife live in Clive, Iowa.

Appendix H: Sources Cited

Chapter 1: Who is Matthew G. Whitaker?

1. Gross, Anthony, The Wit & Wisdom of Abraham Lincoln, Barnes & Noble, 1999, p. 39

2. Frazee, Gretchen, PBS News Hour–Iowa Public Television, November 8, 2018

3. Burke, Michael, "Acting AG incorrectly claimed 'Academic All-American' honors on resume," *Wall Street Journal*, December 26, 2018

4. Goldman, Adman, Michael D. Shear and Mitch Smith, "An Attack Dog With Ambition Beyond Protecting Trump," *New York Times*, November. 9, 2018

5. Hanson, Marc, *The Des Moines Register*, February 1, 2011, p.1B

6. Bronstein, Scott, "Whitaker ran conservative group funded by dark money," CNN, Sunday, November 11, 2018

7. Fein, Bruce, "Whitaker is Unfit to be Attorney General, Acting or Otherwise," *The American Conservative*, November 19, 2018

8. *Wikipedia*, "Matthew Whitaker"

9. Fein, Bruce, "Whitaker is Unfit to be Attorney General, Acting or Otherwise," *The American Conservative*, November 19, 2018

10. Gruber-Miller, Stephen, "To Matt Whitaker, the law--and politics--are 'contact sports,'" *The Des Moines Register*, November 17, 2018

11. Stern, Michael, "A former prosecutor's satirical 'thanks' to President Trump for appointing Matt Whitaker," *The Des Moines Register*, November 16, 2018

12. Gruber-Miller, Stephen, "To Matt Whitaker, the law--and politics--are 'contact sports,'" *The Des Moines Register*, November 17, 2018

13. ibid

14. ibid

15. *Des Moines Register*, November 8, 2018

16. Christian Conservative Family Leader Debate, 2014

17. Fein, Bruce, "Whitaker is Unfit to be Attorney General, Acting or Otherwise: Beyond the unconstitutionality of his

appointment, his views on judicial review and religious litmus tests should disqualify him," *The American Conservative*, November 19, 2018

18. *Wikipedia*, "Dismissal of U.S. Attorneys Controversy"

19. Cohen, Adam, "Woman Wrongly Convicted and a U.S. Attorney Who Kept His Job," <u>Opinion</u> *New York Times*, Editorial Observer, April 16, 2007, Madison, Wisconsin

20. Krugman, Paul, "Department of Injustice," *New York Times*, March 9, 2007

21. Cranberg, Gilbert, 21, "Editorial," *The Des Moines Register*, November 2, 2007

22. Mathews, Susan C., "Letter to Editor," *Green Bay Press-Gazette*, Sheboygan, April 17, 2007

23. *Cap Times*, Editorial: "The sad fate of Steven Biskupic," June 3, 2010

24. Cohen, Adam, "Woman Wrongly Convicted and a U.S. Attorney Who Kept His Job," <u>Opinion</u> *New York Times*, Editorial Observer, April 16, 2007, Madison, Wisconsin

25. Deace, Steve, "Deace in the Afternoon Radio Talk Show," Friday, March 26, 2007

26. Rachel Maddow Show, "MSNBC Transcript," January 28, 2019

27. Woods, Chris, "Political Forecast," Blog, March 24, 2007

28. Harkin, Senator, Tom, E-mail to Jim Ferguson, May 23, 2007

29. Gruber-Miller, Stephen, Op.cit

30. Gruber-Miller, Stephen, Op.cit

31. *Chicago Free Press*, June 18, 2008

32. Baragona, Justin, *Daily Beast*, February 8, 2019

Chapter 3: Not What I Expected: *Bio, Politics, Addiction, Orientation*

33. McCoy, Matt & Jim Ferguson. <u>McCoy, You're Going Straight to Hell: Heartfelt Letters to a Gay State Senator on Marriage Equality</u>, Virtual Bookworm Publishing, Inc., 2014, p. 15

34. Witosky, Tom & Marc Hansen, <u>Equal Before the Law: How Iowa Led Americans to Marriage Equality</u>, University of Iowa Press, Iowa City 2015, p 60

35. Witosky, Tom & Marc Hansen, <u>Equal Before the Law: How Iowa Led Americans to Marriage Equality</u>, University of Iowa Press, Iowa City 2015, p 62

36. Hoffman-Zinnel, Daniel, "Resilient Leadership: A case Study about A Gay Man's Journey of Coming out and Running for Public Office," Doctorial Dissertation, Creighton University, 2015, p. 14

Chapter 4: What Happened

37. Keilar, Brianna, CNN News, April 4, 2019

38. CBS, "Eye on America," July 15, 2005

39. KCCI, "Senator Plans to Push Elderly Home Monitor System," September 28, 2005

Chapter 5: Indictment

40. Ferguson, Jim, "McCoy investigation a misuse of power, money," *Letter to The Des Moines Register,* March 5, 2007

41. *The Des Moines Register,* front page headline, on March 13, 2007

42. Eckhoff, Jeff, "McCoy is charged with extortion D.M. legislator accused of using his position to demand money," *The Des Moines Register*, March 15, 2007, p. 1A

43. Yepsen, David, *The Des Moines Register*, March 15, 2007

44. Duffy, Brian, "Duffy Whitaker Cartoon," *The Des Moines Register*, March 16, 2007 (Original cartoon owned by Matt McCoy and published with permission of cartoonist.)

45. MSNBC.com, "Lawmakers warn FBI on spying powers: Agency told it could lose broad spying authority after revelations of abuses," *The Associated Press*, March 20, 2007

46. Fine, Glenn A., "Statement to the House Judiciary Committee," *Associated Press,* March 20, 2007

47. United States District Court for the Southern District of Iowa Central Division, "Case 4:07-or-0077-JEG-CFB Document 96," Filed 11/27/2077

48. Whitaker, Matthew G. and Mary C. Luxa, "Government's Memorandum in Resistance to Defendant's Motion for Bill of Particulars," May 14, 2007

49. Whitaker, Matthew G. and Mary C. Luxa, "Government's Memorandum in Resistance to Defendant's Motion for Bill of Particulars," May 14, 2007

50. *The Des Moines Register,* "Metro Communities," June 7, 2007

51. Brown, F. Montgomery, "Defendant McCoy's 'Motion to Compel Disclosure,'" November 9, 2007

52. United States District Court for the Southern District of Iowa Central Division, "No. 4:07-cr-0077-JEG, United States of America, Plaintiff, vs. Matthew William McCoy, Defendant," ORDER, filed 11/27/2007

53. Eckhoff, Jeff, *The Des Moines Register*, November 27, 2007

54. Roos, Jonathan, "GOP wants McCoy off committees," *The Des Moines Register,* March 18, 2007, p. 3B

Chapter 6: Trial – Whitaker's role in an assault on our democracy

55. DOJ Website, Department of Integrity Section

56. Basu, Rekha, Columnist, *The Des Moines Register,* December 21, 2007

57. Eckhoff, Jeff, *The Des Moines Register*, December 14, 2007

Chapter 7: Whitaker's Assault on Democracy

58. McCoy, Mathew, "I was the Subject of a Political 'Witch Hunt,' Matt Whitaker Directed it" POLITICO, November 11, 2018

59. Cranberg, Gilbert, *The Des Moines Register*, November 2, 2007

60. Goldman, Adam, Michael D. Shear and Mitch Smith, "Matthew Whitaker: An attack Dog with Ambition Beyond Protecting Trump," *New York Times*, November 9, 2018

61. Hansen, Marc, "Politics fueled McCoy Trial, some say," *The Des Moines Register,* December 20, 2007

62. Basu, Rekha, Columnist, *The Des Moines Register,* December 21, 2007

63. Cranberg, Gilbert, *Cityview,* January 17, 2008

64. Cranberg, Gilbert, *"Government should compensate McCoy for legal fees," Cityview*, January 17, 2008

65. Poem *Richard Cory* by Edwin Arlington Robinson

Made in the USA
Lexington, KY
11 December 2019